THE ROOTS
OF WHO WE ARE

Roots of Youth Ministry Series

This series addresses ecumenical and uniquely Presbyterian youth ministry concerns. Volumes in this series are intended for both professional and lay adults engaged in youth ministry.

Series Writers
Rodger Nishioka
Bob Tuttle
Lynn Turnage

Series Editor
Faye Burdick

Titles In Series
The Roots of Who We Are
Surveying the Land
Dealing with Crisis
Rooted in Love
Sowing the Seeds
Growing Leaders
Growing a Group

The Roots
of Who We Are

Rodger Nishioka

Bridge Resources
Louisville, Kentucky

© 1997 Bridge Resources, Louisville, Kentucky

Scripture quotations in this publication are from the New Revised Standard Version of the Bible, copyright 1989 by the Division of Christian Education of the National Council of the Churches of Christ in the United States of America. In some instances, the text is slightly altered in the interest of inclusive language. Used by permission.

Every effort has been made to trace copyrights on the materials included in this book. If any copyrighted material has nevertheless been included without permission and due acknowledgment, proper credit will be inserted in future printings after notice has been received.

Edited by Faye Burdick
Book interior and cover design by Pamela Ullman

First edition

Published by Bridge Resources
Louisville, Kentucky

PRINTED IN THE UNITED STATES OF AMERICA

ISBN 1-57895-007-4

With deep appreciation and love to the Nishioka family:
Mom, Dad, Jason, Garfield, Michele, and Brandon.

Contents

Acknowledgments

Some time ago there was an article in the Louisville, Kentucky, newspaper, *The Courier-Journal*, that quoted a gentleman who was retiring from many years of work. When the reporter asked the man to reflect on his years of working, he said all he had been doing was "drinking from his saucer." He explained that his cup had been filled to overflowing so much that all he had been able to do was lift the cup and drink the overflow from the saucer. I know how he feels.

In September 1996, I completed ten years of service as the associate for youth ministry with the General Assembly Council of the Presbyterian Church (U.S.A.). Throughout those ten years, I was privileged to spend time with thousands of wonderful young people and adults. Early on, youth and adults alike began to encourage me to share some of my thoughts through writing. I balked at the suggestion, not believing much of anything I had to share was worthy of print. It was not until my colleagues and close friends, Bob Tuttle and Lynn Turnage, talked with me about teaming up that I even began to consider the idea of writing a book for Presbyterians about youth ministry. And even then I didn't take it seriously until Faye Burdick, our remarkable editor for this series, seized upon the idea and encouraged us with great enthusiasm. So now you hold in your hands my humble (truly!) attempt to provide some clarity and support to the challenge and gift that is ministry with young people.

I am so grateful to Lynn and Bob for their friendship and collegiality. I am grateful to Faye Burdick for her excellent editing and to colleagues and friends in the Congregational Ministries Division of the General Assembly Council for their support. I am especially grateful to Robert Miller for his decision to issue me the call to serve in 1986, to Don Brown, Marvin Simmers, Eunice Poethig, and Ed Craxton for their care and support of our church's ministry with young people and their kindness and friendship with me in particular. Finally, I owe much to the youth and adults of the Presbyterian Church (U.S.A.), who have been so welcoming and gracious in sharing so much of their lives with me. My hope and fervent prayer is that this series of resources might provide some sustenance for this vital ministry with our young people and their families, and I give thanks to God for the opportunity to be connected to so many through the work of the Holy Spirit. I have moved to a new area of responsibility in ministry with young adults. And I have a hunch that through the grace of our Lord Jesus Christ, I'm going to keep on keeping on . . . drinking from my saucer.

Rodger Nishioka

1
Reformed Theology

Elena flinched when she heard the question from her friend Sara. "Where were you this weekend?" Sara asked. "I tried all weekend to get a hold of you."

Oh," muttered Elena, "I was busy."

"Well, duh," said Sara. "Where were you?"

"I was at a retreat for my church," said Elena.

Sara wrinkled her face. "A church retreat?" she asked. "Did you have fun?"

"Well, it was OK," said Elena.

"What church do you go to?" asked Sara.

"The Presbyterian one," said Elena.

"Presbyterian? What's a Presbyterian?" asked Sara.

"Oh, I don't know," said Elena. "All I know is that we sprinkle people with water instead of dunking them, and we say 'debts' instead of 'trespasses' when we pray the Lord's Prayer."

Whether she knew it or not, Elena pretty well summed up what most young people think about being Presbyterian. Another popular answer I've received when I have asked young people what it means to be "Presbyterian" is that no one can "spell us." But given a long and faithful heritage of people who have helped form what it means to be Presbyterian, these answers are far from adequate. Why is it even important to talk about being Presbyterian and Reformed?

Three Major Reasons

First, it's important that we talk about being Presbyterian because that's who we are. God is not a look-alike God. Just glance around you while in the midst of a crowd of people. God's creativity is evident! Clearly, God is not interested in uniform thinking and uniform worshiping. The idea that God calls each of us to worship is essential. God calls faithful Christians to be Presbyterians and Baptists and Methodists and Roman Catholics and the list goes on. Our task is to be the most faithful Presbyterian we can be—not at the expense of our Christian traditions, but to enhance the experience of other Christian traditions. In other words, God is a Baskin-Robbins® God who loves different flavors of worship. As Presbyterians, we are called to be the best-flavored Presbyterians in the bunch!

Second, young people in our congregations are going to run into young people from other Christian traditions and non-Christians who at some point will ask why they go to a Presbyterian church or what it means to be Presbyterian. We do a disservice to our young people when we don't help them formulate a response. We can help them formulate a response by helping them understand more about being Presbyterian.

Third, when a young child asks a parent about heaven or God, she is already thinking "theologically," that is, about how God is active in the world and relates to the world. But for too many of us, doing theology is somehow stunted. When we talk about what it means to be Presbyterian, we are helping young people grow theologically and hone their skills in looking for how God is interacting with the world and articulating what they are seeing. This is one of the great gifts and one of the great challenges of youth ministry! So what does it mean to be Presbyterian?

As Presbyterians, we belong to the particular group of churches known as the "Reformed" churches. These churches grew out of the Reformation movement in Switzerland that was emerging simultaneously with the Reformation movement in Germany led by Martin Luther. The Swiss Reformers were led first by Ulrich Zwingli in Zurich and then later by William Farel and John Calvin in Geneva. Initially, Zwingli and Luther agreed on many of the same points. Divergence came, however, when Zwingli and later Farel and Calvin moved the focus of worship away from the Eucharist to the preaching of the Word. Reformed Christians believe the Eucharist is a symbolic remembrance of the life, death, and resurrection of Christ. Lutherans continue to focus more on the Eucharist and believe that the essence of the blood and body of Christ is somehow present in the elements. Roman Catholics, Eastern Orthodox, and Episcopalian Christians believe that in the Eucharist, the bread and wine are transformed into the body and blood of Christ, not merely symbols. Of the Reformed leaders, John Calvin is best known because he wrote the *Institutes of the Christian Religion*, a series of four books that discusses how a Christian gains a knowledge of God the Creator and God the Redeemer in Christ, how a Christian obtains the grace of Christ, and the role of the holy catholic Church in this process. Calvin was also instrumental in creating the Presbyterian style of governance, with the session (or consistory), the presbytery (or colloquy), the provincial synod, and the national synod (or General Assembly). Other Reformed churches in the United States include the Reformed Church in America, the United Church of Christ, the Christian Church (Disciples of Christ), the Evangelical Presbyterian Church, the Presbyterian Church in America, and the Cumberland Presbyterian Church.

Based on the writings of Calvin and other theologians, I want to propose five key tenets of Reformed theology. I am indebted to my friend and colleague, the Rev. Dr. Frank Hainer, a longtime editor of our fine adult study resources, for this outline that he shared with me and many others several years ago at an educators' conference.

❦

Tenet One: Presbyterians hold up the sovereignty of God.

Let us use great caution that neither our thoughts nor our speech go beyond the limits to which the Word of God itself extends. For how can the human mind measure off the measureless essence of God according to its own little measure, a mind as yet unable to establish for certain the nature of the sun's body, though men's eyes daily gaze upon it? Indeed, how can the mind by its own leading come to search out God's essence when it cannot even get to its own? Let us then willingly leave to God the knowledge of himself.[1]

—John Calvin's *Institutes*

❦

Presbyterians have no problem with mystery and God. It makes sense to us that because God is greater than all that we are, we cannot possibly begin to understand or know all that God is. This basic understanding leads us to the key tenet of the sovereignty of God. Put simply, God is God and there is no other. Presbyterians work hardest at reminding ourselves and others that God is ultimately in control and that there is nothing we can do to control God in any way. Further, because God is so much greater than we are, we cannot possibly know all that God knows or understand all that God is. Therefore, we are called to trust and to believe. We stand against other Christian traditions that somehow claim to have some power over God. For instance, most Presbyterians don't have a prayer of "invocation" in our worship because the very idea that we could somehow invoke God to be present in our worship is preposterous! Instead, we begin with a call to worship to remind us that we are worshiping the one true God, so we are to listen up and pay attention! Reformed theology reminds us that God is the first actor in our relationship with God, that nothing we do or do not do constricts God's actions in any way. God acts first in giving us Jesus Christ. God acts first in showing us grace. God acts first in sustaining us through the Holy Spirit. Our response is to receive Christ as our Lord and Savior and live accordingly. Our response is to grow as a disciple. Our response is to seek the leading of the Holy Spirit.

What does this mean for us?

1. We see worship as the heart of our tradition.

We come to worship not for ourselves but because the one who made us and redeemed us and sustains us is so amazing and great that we can do nothing else *but* worship God! I cringe when I hear someone say they "just don't get anything out of worship because it's so boring." We are so self-centered! The act of worship is not about our being bored or not being bored. The act of worship is a response to God's amazing grace shown to us in Jesus Christ. We can only hope that God is not bored!

2. We emphasize the God of the Trinity.

We focus on God the Creator, the father and mother of us all, who is uniquely revealed to us in Jesus Christ and is present through the Holy Spirit. We focus on the God of the Trinity. If we just focus on God as the historical Creator, we risk a faith that has little to do with us now. If we just focus on God in Jesus Christ, we risk a faith that is based on sentimentalism and dismisses the history of God's relationships with the Hebrew people. If we just focus on the Holy Spirit, we risk a faith that leads to mysticism and discounts all of God's activity. Therefore, we focus on the God of the Trinity.

3. We worship a God who is with us now, present and active in our lives.

Several years ago, Bette Midler, a popular vocalist, sang a hit song titled "From a Distance." The chorus for the song indicated that God is watching us from a distance. Nice song but lousy theology for Presbyterians because it stops short and gives the impression that God is only watching us from somewhere out there. A Presbyterian version of the song would say that God is watching us from a distance and from within our midst because God is sovereign and is everywhere. How dare we try to constrain God to a distant watching place! God chose to become human in Jesus Christ. God chose to be with us then and is with us now through the Holy Spirit.

What does this look like in youth ministry?

Youth ministry leaders need to work hard to remind ourselves that God is in control. Youth ministry is not simply up to us. We're not here to be *all* for these young people. God is at work in us. God is in control. But we need to be careful about how we interpret God's sovereignty to young people. Too many young people have gotten the message that since God is in control, God *causes* people to die and God *wants* accidents to happen. Our theology of God's sovereignty reminds us that God is all-powerful, but, in God's power, God has allowed human beings to make choices. Our emphasis on God's sovereignty helps us trust that even in the struggles of our lives, God is with us and that, ultimately, all things do work together for good for those who love God and are called to God's purpose *(Rom. 8:28)*.

❧

Tenet Two: Presbyterians are formed and reformed by God's Word in Scripture.

Let this be a firm principle: No other word is to be held as the Word of God, and given place as such in the church, than what is contained first in the Law and the Prophets, then in the writings of the apostles; and the only authorized way of teaching in the church is by the prescription and standard of his Word.[2]

—John Calvin's *Institutes*

❦

For Scripture is the school of the Holy Spirit, in which, as nothing is omitted that is both necessary and useful to know, so nothing is taught but what is expedient to know.[3]

—John Calvin's *Institutes*

❦

Because of our roots in the Swiss reformers, Presbyterians are also known as "the people of the Word." For us, theology possesses the key task of interpreting the biblical message. Calvin introduced the idea of commentaries to help prepare us for the reading of the *Word*, and he began teaching the Scriptures to everyone so that all might be able to read and discuss the Bible and its meaning. It is no accident that Presbyterians ordain women and men to the ministry of the *Word* and Sacrament. God's Word found in Scripture is primary. For us, the preaching and teaching of the Word is the focus of our lives. But the Bible does not stand alone. We believe that the Holy Spirit is active in revealing God's word to us. For Presbyterians, then, no one has the corner on truth. We reject the notion that a pope or a bishop or an executive presbyter or moderator or stated clerk or even a pastor gains God's revelation more than any other member of Christ's church. For us, when a pastor preaches, he or she is opening the Scripture up to us for further reading and understanding through the leading of the Holy Spirit. We believe that in the very act of preaching, the Holy Spirit is helping us understand more of God's word.

What does this mean for us?

1. We find the authority of Christ in Scripture.

For Presbyterians, we believe the Bible holds the authority of Christ. These are not just stories about a nice person. Christ's identity as the Son of God comes to us through Scripture. That is why in order to know Christ, we must know Scripture. One of the key ideas of Scripture is the sinfulness of humankind. There is no question that we often do not love, reconcile, or act as conduits of justice and peace. Presbyterians are not surprised by evil in the world, but we are less inclined to give credit to the person of Satan and more inclined to say this is further evidence of our "total depravity" and, therefore, our need for God's grace.

2. We believe in the God of the Bible.

While we struggle with some of the texts in Scripture, we do not discount them, nor do we worship or venerate the Bible as some other Christian traditions do. We do believe that God's greatest revelation is found in the New Testament in Jesus Christ, but that does not mean we dismiss the Old Testament. We do understand that God's Word as expressed in Scripture stands in a historical setting, so we pay particular attention to context to gain meaning. Even more, we rely on the Holy Spirit to help us understand Scripture in our context today.

3. We are more interested in the spirit of Scripture than the letter of Scripture.

Presbyterians are not literalists. While we focus on the Word, we do not do so literally. Because we take Scripture in context, we seek to understand what Scripture meant to the original writers and the original readers and hearers. Such an understanding then informs our understanding today. God's word always stands in history but is in no way bound by history. That words written almost 2,000 years ago still have relevance and profound meaning for us today we believe is a sign of the work of the Holy Spirit—and still more evidence of God's faithfulness to us.

What does this look like in youth ministry?

We have to engage young people in regular Bible study. It is a tragedy that so many youth and adults are biblically illiterate. We cannot possibly know God's revelation without spending time knowing God's Word. Sadly, say the words "Bible study" to young people and they conjure up a scene of being lectured to by someone. That's not it! Certainly there is a role for teaching the basics about the

Bible, but nothing demonstrates the excitement and the importance of the Scripture like a small group Bible study. Plan for a small group to spend six to eight sessions together looking at a particular set of stories or a book in the Bible. Start by offering this as optional in addition to all that you're doing. Offer the in-depth study twice a year. Don't worry if only two or three are interested. Start with them. Remember, God is at work! There are many good resources available. Chapter 6 suggests a process for studying the Bible.

❦

Tenet Three: Presbyterians focus more on glorifying God and the coming of God's reign than the saving of souls.

For so he [Paul] speaks to the Romans: 'All have sinned and lack the glory of God; moreover, they are justified freely by his grace.' Here you have the head and primal source: that God embraced us with his free mercy.[4]

—John Calvin's *Institutes*

❦

For we have it from the words of the apostle that the salvation of believers has been founded upon the decision of divine election alone, and that this favor is not earned by works but comes from free calling.[5]

—John Calvin's *Institutes*

❦

Presbyterians, for better or for worse, are associated with the doctrine of predestination. Although Luther agreed with this doctrine also, the label has been given most often to Presbyterians. For Reformed Christians, the doctrine states that God has chosen (or elected) some to faith. While many Reformed Christians struggle with this doctrine, it is clearly a part of our faith heritage. For Reformed Christians,

The Roots of Who We Are

salvation is not something to be earned. Salvation is a gift from God. It is a gift to all. But for reasons only God knows (predestined?), certain people will receive the gift, and others will reject it. Historically, then, because salvation is God's gift, Presbyterians have been concerned more with glorifying God and bringing about God's reign than with saving souls. After all, we don't save—only God can save. Tragically, some have interpreted this stand to mean that we do not offer young people the opportunity to receive Christ as Lord and Savior. Not true! We do offer opportunities for commitment and recommitment, but because of God's sovereignty, we are wary of those traditions that seem to say that a commitment to Christ is an *individual's* decision, as though God has nothing to do with it. We talk more about this in Chapter 5, on evangelism and young people.

What does this mean for us?

1. We see our first task as glorifying God.

While we offer young people opportunities to commit their lives to Christ, we do so knowing that God is at work in all our lives and that any commitment is not an end-all in itself but one step in the journey called faithfulness and discipleship. Presbyterians are notorious for being involved in the community and for trying to bring about changes in government and in society. We are active being the church today for all people. Calvin transformed the city of Geneva and dedicated the last chapter of his final book to the Christian's relationship to the civil magistrates.

2. We trust in God's sovereignty.

Sound familiar? It should! Salvation truly is God's gift. There is nothing we can do to earn it. A good friend of mine from another faith tradition has little stick figures he has drawn on the inside cover of his Bible. Each figure, he explained to me, represents people he "has saved." Needless to say, we've had long discussions about his theology of salvation. Presbyterians believe that we don't save; only God saves. Our job is to be faithful. Surely we offer opportunities for young people to receive Christ as Lord and Savior and surely we offer opportunities for young people (and adults and children) to rededicate their lives to Christ, but salvation is up to God. Salvation does not depend upon our understanding. That's why infant baptism makes so much sense for us. Baptism for us is a sign of God's saving love shown to us in Jesus Christ. It is not dependent on our understanding or the infant's confession. It is dependent on God, who acted first!

3. We see faith as a response to God's grace.

We live faithfully not to earn God's grace but in response to it. Frank Hainer, whom I mentioned earlier, says that other traditions around us are bad news—good news people. The bad news is that you are a sinner. The good news is that if you work hard enough, God will save you. In contrast, we Presbyterians are good news —bad news people. The good news is that God saves you. The bad news is that you have to be good anyway. We do not live as disciples so that we will be saved. Our salvation is intact. God has chosen us already and nothing we do can change that. Our response to God's amazing love is to live a life faithful to God out of gratitude.

What does this look like in youth ministry?
Your goal is not to "save" these young people. Your goal is to be faithful as a disciple of Jesus Christ. One young person told me she stopped going to her church youth group because she felt like she was letting her advisors down by not believing everything they said. Clearly, the Holy Spirit was at work in her, and she was struggling with forming her own beliefs—a vital step in her faith journey! But the message she was getting from her advisors was "you have to believe what we believe to make us feel good about you!" Arrrgh! Our task is to trust that God really is at work. Our task is to pray constantly for young people and their families. Our task is to be available to them. So let's be open to the questioning and the wondering. In those questions, a lifelong faith in Jesus Christ is being formed!

❦

Tenet Four: Presbyterians believe the church is the Holy Community.

From this the face of the church comes forth and becomes visible to our eyes. Wherever we see the Word of God purely preached and heard, and the sacraments administered according to Christ's institution, there, it is not to be doubted, a church of God exists. For [God's] promise cannot fail: "Wherever two or three are gathered in my name, there I am in the midst of them."[6]

—John Calvin's *Institutes*

❦

Presbyterians believe you cannot be a faithful Christian on your own. Other traditions focus only on a person's relationship with God or their believing in Jesus Christ. We focus on that relationship, too, but we also focus on the relationship of the believer to their community. Years ago when I was questioning my Dad, himself a Presbyterian pastor, as to whether or not people could be Christians on their own, he told me that we as Presbyterians believe that when we gather for worship, we are not only the body of Christ but the best expression of Christ on the face of the earth. Calvin deemed the church the "Holy Community," and while we are far from perfect, we still need each other to keep accountable as disciples of Jesus Christ. I am so encouraged when I encounter a congregation that seeks to include everyone in all aspects of worship. Worship really is the essence of who we are, and it is not right that our children or young people should be excluded. We need each other to be the holy community of Christ!

What does this mean for us?

1. We believe God's call comes both personally and corporately.

Our theology of call is measured both by the individual's affirmation and by the community's affirmation. Other traditions rely only on the individual even if the community disagrees. For Presbyterians, any call must be validated by both the individual and the community. That's why, for instance, when a person feels called to serve as a minister of the Word and Sacrament, they must be taken under the care of the session. In doing so, the congregation affirms the call of the individual and agrees to support them as they continue to discern the Holy Spirit's leading.

2. We are committee people.

For better or for worse, we love committees. But committees for Presbyterians are not a cop-out or a stalling tactic (although they may sometimes feel that way!). Rather, they are an expression of our theology. Since community is so important, we do everything in groups. The idea of one person, like the pope or an archbishop, who receives a revelation from God alone and then passes it on to the people, makes no sense for us. We need each other to discern what God is saying to us. In Bible study, in governance, in worship, we need each other. We believe we are enhanced and even more faithful when we gather together. The sin for Presbyterians is to enter a group with your mind made up. In doing so, you are closing yourself to the work of the Holy Spirit through sisters and brothers.

3. We are a connected people.

Connection continues to be an important word for Presbyterians. Other Christians are amazed at our elaborate church structures. Some traditions are loosely joined as federations with each congregation pretty much operating on their own. We're unique in that we participate in each governing body in our congregations, presbyteries, synods, and the General Assembly. No one part dominates any of the others and all are needed in order for all of us to be connected. And while there are a variety of worship styles and even theological stances in our congregations, we all are connected through the Holy Spirit.

What does this look like in youth ministry?

For young people, community is key. We build community constantly because God has created us to be a relational people, and adolescents of all age groups resonate with this need most of all. But we who are adults are also a crucial part of the community. We must work to combat the rampant individualism of our age that tells young people that it's all up to them. We must help young people see that we are the body of Christ and connected to each other. Being a Christian is not just a "me and Jesus" journey. Being a Christian is about being a part of a Christian community. Our theology is lived out in our sanctuaries and worship spaces. Presbyterians don't have an altar. We have a Communion Table around which all the people of God gather. What a powerful symbol of our theology! Anything you can do, from postcards to T-shirts to attending concerts and games to mission trips, to help nurture the belonging and accountability of community will help.

❦

Tenet Five: Presbyterians engage our mind and will for God's glory.

To sum up: We see among all [human]kind that reason is proper to our nature; it distinguishes us from brute beasts, just as they by possessing feeling differ from inanimate things.[7]

—John Calvin's *Institutes*

❦

For it always follows that nothing good can arise out of our will until it has been reformed; and after its reformation, in so far as it is good, it is so from God, not from ourselves.[8]

—John Calvin's *Institutes*

❦

In the dead of winter, I had just arrived at a hotel in Buffalo to speak at a youth rally for Western New York Presbytery. As I was unpacking, I found myself out of shaving cream. I called the front desk, and they sent me to a gas station a few blocks away. I trudged through the snow and got to the gas station. Sure enough, the clerk, a woman probably in her sixties, kindly pulled a can of shaving cream from the shelf in her plexiglass–protected booth. She asked if I drove and I explained that I was at the hotel nearby. When she asked what I was doing in Buffalo, I told her about my work. Since I was preaching on Sunday, I invited her to join us for worship. I remember her reaction vividly. She scoffed and said, "I can't go to a Presbyterian Church! I'm not smart enough!"

Presbyterians are known as thinking people. Some say that we think too much. Calvin was clearly an academician. He is famous for being the first theologian to write such a comprehensive system of theology in his *Institutes*. We Reformed Christians have reflected his academics ever since. In fact, Presbyterians require extensive theological work of our candidates for ordination to the ministry of the Word and Sacrament. All of this reflects on engaging our mind and will for God's glory.

What does this mean for us?

1. We study a lot.

A good friend who is a Southern Baptist told me that we Presbyterians try to think our way to God. She's right in many ways. We sometimes neglect the feeling side of our faith, and while we're loosening up some, we're still afraid of the easy sentimentalism of some other Christian traditions. But the good news about Presbyterians that even my Southern Baptist friend acknowledged is that we tend to build our faith and trust more on our certainty and knowledge of God's faithfulness rather than our feeling of God's faithfulness. This is reflected powerfully in our *Book of Confessions*. This book of eleven creeds, catechisms, and confessional documents from the ancient Nicene Creed to the modern Brief Statement of Faith, provides both a basic understanding of what the Presbyterian Church (U.S.A.) has believed through its history, as well as a dramatic picture of how the Holy Spirit is leading the church. The eleven documents form the first part of our Constitution with the *Book of Order* being the second part.

2. We do things decently and in order.

The old denominational joke goes something like this: When God organizes a worship service, God puts the Episcopalians in charge of the processional and recessional, the Baptists in charge of the preaching and the praying, the Methodists in charge of the music, and the Presbyterians in charge of ushering and collecting and counting the offering. We do like to do things decently and in order. That's given us a bad reputation as the "frozen chosen." But while we may not be the picture of spontaneity, there are reasons for our orderliness. Our theology of engaging the mind and will for God's glory means we must be deliberate and disciplined about being the faithful together. People have to follow through with responsibilities. Make no mistake, however, that many congregations are very fluid in their worship and even in their session meetings!

3. We tend to be critical of government.

Because we are thinking people, we are always calling ourselves and our government to the highest good. Presbyterians are known for being aware of what is happening and trying to defend the defenseless. Calvin urged Reformed Christians to be aware of what is happening in their government and in the world around them. Sadly, the church has not always lived up to this role. But the Reformed church view is to be engaged in the world, not to shy away from it. Other traditions try to pull their people away from the world and its challenges. Presbyterians, with a great history of mission and missionary movements, have long been involved in the world hoping to transform it.

What does this look like in youth ministry?

Many are familiar with a personality assessment tool named the Myers-Briggs Type Indicator (MBTI). The MBTI assesses personalities in eight categories. Two of them are feelers versus thinkers. Feeling types are more emotive, while thinking types are more logical. While the MBTI estimates that half the general population are feelers and half are thinkers, there is good evidence to indicate that a majority of young people are more feelers than thinkers. This means that while Presbyterians like to think, many Presbyterian young people are more interested in feeling than thinking about their faith. Leaders, then, need to provide more than equal time for feelers to express their faith through music, drama, poetry, and art. At the same time, however, thinkers need to be able to think through their faith. Look through your activities to be sure you have a balance of both. It will help tremendously if the leadership, both adults and young people, are both feelers and thinkers. Remember that we all have both thinking and feeling abilities inside us.

2
Reformed or
Not Reformed?

Now that you're an expert on Reformed theology (I know, I know. We're all still learning. Don't worry!), here's a quiz. Ideally, it would be best if you worked this through with a group of other leaders. (Remember we seek God's guidance in community!) These are all real statements I've heard from young people. You decide if each one is "R" for Reformed, "B" for borderline, or "N" for Not Reformed. My responses are on the page following the reproducible quiz.

Quiz

1. Basically, I think all people are good; we just make poor choices sometimes.

   R ☐ B ☐ N ☐

2. The ultimate decision for what you should do with your life rests with you. I mean, get advice and pray and all that, but it's up to *you* to decide.

   R ☐ B ☐ N ☐

3. God speaks when you are still enough to listen.   R ☐ B ☐ N ☐

4. Certainly we go to church to worship and praise God, but it's also important that the church meet your needs—you know, do something for you. If you don't get something out of it, why go?   R ☐ B ☐ N ☐

5. Jesus is all that I need to get through life.   R ☐ B ☐ N ☐

6. The Bible says it. I believe it. That settles it.   R ☐ B ☐ N ☐

7. Like the song says, we have to do what's right because   R ☐ B ☐ N ☐ "God is watching us from a distance."

8. It was so cool. God knew I was in this incredible hurry to get to class, and so he gave me a parking space right in front of school. I just love it when God takes care of me like that!   R ☐ B ☐ N ☐

9. You have to believe in yourself. If you don't believe in yourself, no one else will believe in you.   R ☐ B ☐ N ☐

10. You don't really have to go to church to be a Christian. At least not all the time.   R ☐ B ☐ N ☐

11. I don't see how being a Christian has anything to do with the government. I mean, what about the separation of church and state?   R ☐ B ☐ N ☐

12. If you're going to talk the talk, you have to walk the walk.   R ☐ B ☐ N ☐

13. I've saved four people by leading them to profess their faith in Jesus as their Lord and Savior.   R ☐ B ☐ N ☐

14. My mind is made up because God told me so.   R ☐ B ☐ N ☐

15. We've always done it that way before.   R ☐ B ☐ N ☐

16. You need to trust the Holy Spirit more rather than trying to study and analyze everything. Your problem is you try to think your way to God rather than feel God.   R ☐ B ☐ N ☐

17. I just don't feel good enough that Jesus would die for me. I know I was baptized as a baby and I was confirmed last year and I've received Christ as my Lord and Savior several times and once I even went forward at a Billy Graham crusade thing, but I mess up all the time and I just don't think I'm good enough. I'm afraid I won't go to heaven.   R ☐ B ☐ N ☐

My Responses

1. *Not Reformed.* We believe that while God created all people good, *Rom. 3:23* reminds us that all have sinned and fallen short of the glory of God. If we were not sinners, why would we need God's grace in Jesus Christ? Reformed Christians recognize the sinfulness of humankind. But what about children and especially infants who die during childbirth or in the days following their birth? Does that mean they are going to hell? Calvin says certainly not!

❦

[God] will be our God and the God of our descendants after us. Their salvation is embraced in this word. No one will dare be so insolent toward God as to deny that [God's] promise of itself suffices for its effect.[1]

—John Calvin's *Institutes*

❦

2. *Not Reformed.* Certainly you are accountable for your own actions, but language here is far too individualistic. We believe the call comes both personally and corporately. In the Westminster Confession of Faith in our *Book of Confessions* (6.109), we read that "God alone is Lord of the Conscience," but that does not give permission for individuals to do whatever they please. The rest of the phrase reads, "and hath left it free from the doctrines and commandments of men which are in anything contrary to his Word, or beside it in matters of faith and worship." This is further evidence that our actions are guided by the Word of God and the worshiping community.

3. *Not Reformed.* This is a challenge to God's sovereignty. God speaks whether we are still or not. Our job is to always be ready and listening.

4. *Not Reformed.* The first question and answer in the Shorter Catechism in the *Book of Confessions* (7.001) is this: "What is the chief end of [humankind]? [Humankind's] chief end is to glorify God, and to enjoy [God] forever." It says nothing about our getting anything out of the relationship. Our job is to worship God. The grace we experience in this is that hopefully we *do* get something out of it, but that's not why we go to church!

5. *Not Reformed.* Certainly this is partially true, but Reformed Christians look at the God of the Trinity. John Calvin said that God was "fully present in Jesus Christ but not limited by Christ." So God is Christ but at the same time is more than Christ. God is the Holy Spirit but at the same time is more than the Holy Spirit.

6. *Not Reformed.* Far too simplistic and too individualistic. How do you know what the Bible says? There is no such thing as pure revelation. All of us bring our experiences and ideas to any reading of the Scripture. That's why Presbyterians read Scripture in community so that we can be helped to discern the leading of the Holy Spirit by brothers and sisters. Unlike our Roman Catholic sisters and brothers, we have no one who is infallible (like the Pope), so we must rely on the leading of the Holy Spirit through each of us. Johanna van Wijk-Bos, an outstanding professor of the Old Testament at Louisville Presbyterian Theological Seminary, writes in her book, *Reformed and Feminist*, "Putting the Bible in the center of belief and practice means that one trusts God to provide a word for our time and perplexity. It may also mean that this word is different from what one expects it to be."[2]

7. *Not Reformed.* God is not only out there somewhere. God is God. God is everywhere! Besides, Christ promised us that God would send the Holy Spirit to be with us. This is a transcendent God who is in our midst.

8. *Borderline.* This is an interesting one. A person with a strict view of predestination would say that God is active in all that happens. Later theologians have tamed that view somewhat to distinguish between God's causative will and God's permissive will. Still, I lean to Not Reformed. I'm uncomfortable with a view of God as a "candy man" where if you ask enough, God will give it to you. What happens the next time you really need a parking place? Or why doesn't God clear the way for that ambulance, and so forth? St. Augustine wrote in the *City of God* that "Christians are distinguished not so much by what happens to them but rather by the way they respond to what happens to them."[3] There is a distinction between God's being with us and for us in all that happens and God's causing all that happens.

9. *Not Reformed.* Again, far too self-centered. The pressure is not just on you. There have been many times the community believed in individuals when they themselves did not. That community belief ended up helping them to survive.

10. *Not Reformed.* Reformed Christians believe you need the community of faith to keep you accountable. Therefore, you may share the gifts the Holy Spirit has given to you. For us, being a Christian is not just the vertical relationship with God; it is the horizontal relationship with the community as well.

11. *Not Reformed.* The separation of church and state is a modern idea. Calvin certainly knew nothing about it. Jesus did say "give to Caesar what is Caesar's and to God what is God's," but he was being questioned by religious leaders who were trying to entrap him into starting a riot against the Roman rulers. Reformed Christians believe that government is instituted by God and, therefore, it is subject to God's rule and must be held accountable.

12. *Reformed.* This is another interesting one. I consider it Reformed in that it holds us accountable to live (or walk) obedient to God even as we talk about obedience. I'm more than a little wary, though, of the always sly concept that somehow we have to be worthy of God's grace; that's why we have to walk the walk. This statement doesn't say that, but I've often heard it used with that overtone.

13. *Not Reformed.* Reformed Christians can lead persons to profess their faith in Christ, but the saving action is God's, not our own. Even more, given our doctrine of predestination and limited election, God has chosen us before we chose God. Again, this is the sovereignty of God.

14. *Not Reformed.* Reformed Christians believe we are being less than faithful when we enter any context with our "mind made up" for whatever reason. We study because we want to be informed, and we discuss because we believe that the Holy Spirit speaks to us in discussion and through prayer and study. No one has a corner on the truth of God's revelation.

15. *Not Reformed.* This may be a typical Presbyterian phrase, but it is not a Reformed one. One of the great phrases of our church is *"Ecclesia Reformandat, Semper Reformata"* (The Reformed Church, Forever Reforming). Phrases like this deny God's sovereignty in that God is always leading us. Who knows what God has in store?

16. *Not Reformed.* However, I could be persuaded to call this one Borderline. My initial reaction is Not Reformed because it dismisses the mind. God gave us minds for a reason. Our job is to use them. We can be indicted, though, for using them at the expense of our feelings. Sometimes, when young people are yearning for the experience of God, we feed them the knowledge of God and wonder what is wrong. Our job is to provide opportunities where the Holy Spirit can work through us and our leadership to give both.

17. *Not Reformed.* But this certainly is very human. This person seems convinced that somehow we can do something to earn God's grace offered to us in Jesus Christ. The truth is that we are not good enough to be saved, and we can never be good enough to be saved. That's what grace is all about. This very question is what started Martin Luther and Ulrich Zwingli on their separate but simultaneous journeys that led to the Reformation. They both asked the question, How can a sinful person be saved by a righteous God? Their answer? Only through God's grace. That's why Reformed Christians, while certainly painfully aware of our sinful state, put so much emphasis on grace. It's God's doing, not our own. John Leith, a retired professor of theology from Union Theological Seminary in Richmond, Virginia, and a great Reformed theologian, wrote in his book *The Reformed Imperative:* "The Reformed witness to the world today is that God's grace is the last word in every human situation whether that situation is a historical event that overwhelms us or a natural event that threatens us with destruction."[4]

How did you do? My hope is that you might use this quiz with young people and other adults. How about a discussion with your elders and deacons? You might even change answers based on good discussions. That's wonderful! Remember, the Holy Spirit is at work!

Questions to Evaluate a Resource

As you consider resources, curriculum, videos, and program designs for your youth ministry, consult the following checklist to be sure the materials you use reflect our Reformed theology.

When looking at God, Jesus Christ, and the Holy Spirit, consider the following:

❦ Is the focus on only one person in the Trinity or is there a balance of all three?

❦ Is God presented as the first and foremost actor whose actions are not dependent on humankind?

❦ Is God presented as transcendent, that is, in our midst?

❦ Is there an emphasis on God's grace rather than the threat of God's judgment?

❦ Is the worship of God presented as the faithful response of the Christian to God's grace?

When looking at the Bible, consider the following:

❦ Is Scripture presented in the context in which it was written? Is the historical situation given?

❦ Is there a balance of Scripture from sections of the Old and New Testaments?

❦ Is the Bible presented as the living Word of God with fresh revelations given to us through the Holy Spirit?

❦ Is the Bible to be studied and read with others?

❦ Are young people encouraged to share and discuss the impact of the text on their lives today?

When looking at salvation and commitment, consider the following:

❦ Is just as much attention given to the nurtured conversion as the dramatic conversion? (For more about this terminology, see chapter 5 on evangelism.)

❦ Is a decision to follow Christ's ways portrayed as a key step in the journey of faith?

❦ Is salvation seen purely as God's grace without any demands or expectations?

❦ Is obedience seen as a response to God's grace rather than an attempt to earn God's grace?

- Are there opportunities for young people who have already committed their life to Christ to take further steps of discipleship?

When looking at the community of faith, consider the following:

- Are there significant community-building activities?
- Are young people encouraged to work in the world to transform the world to God's realm?
- Are young people encouraged to participate fully in the church?
- Is God's call sought and weighed both individually and corporately?
- Is a more individualistic faith reinforced?
- Are there opportunities for the group to connect themselves to the whole church?
- Are there opportunities for the group to connect themselves to the wider community?
- Are there opportunities for the group to connect themselves to the whole world?

When looking at how young people are encouraged to think, consider the following:

- Is there an equal representation of women and men, and are stereotypes for males and females avoided?
- Are young people invited to think critically, or are only right and wrong answers given?
- Are questions open-ended, or do they seek just yes and no answers?
- Is there a balance of thinking and feeling questions and activities?

The following are other issues to consider:

- Are young people portrayed as leaders as well as followers?
- Are youth and adults presented as partners in ministry?
- Are a diversity of young people and adults presented?

3

A Theology of Youth Ministry

Early in my work as a youth leader, several people instilled in my head the idea that if you can possibly avoid it, you *never* cancel an event. I was teaching school in Seattle at the time and was invited to lead a weekend confirmation retreat for a congregation. On Thursday night before that weekend, the pastor called and said nearly everyone had canceled except two of the young people, and he was willing to cancel the event if I wanted to back out. While I could have used the free weekend, I thought better of it and we went. It turned out the ratio was four adults to the two young people. These two young people were on the fringe of the confirmation class and nominal churchgoers. Neither of their families were involved in the congregation. We were at a church member's condo in the mountains, and I reworked all of the activities for four adults and two young people instead of the anticipated four adults and fourteen young people. We ended up having a great day of skiing and inner tubing. We shared faith journeys and sang songs and read the Bible together. Late on Saturday night, all six of us were sitting in the hot tub outside. We were looking up at the stars, and then one of the young people, Kevin, who had been quiet much of the day, turned to me and said, "You know, you really believe this stuff, don't you?" And so began one of the richest and most honest conversations I've experienced about God and Jesus Christ and the Holy Spirit and the church and, well, you get the picture. In that hot tub, all six of us, late at night, were *doing* theology.

In Chapter 1, we began by looking at what it means to be Reformed in theology and what that looks like in youth ministry. As I stated earlier, one of the great privileges and challenges of youth ministry is to help young people hone their skills in thinking theologically and in articulating what they believe. One of the common indictments of those of us who engage in the practical ministries of the church and in youth ministry in particular is that we neither think or talk theologically nor help our young people to think or talk this way. I dispute this indictment.

At the same time, however, I recognize the need for us to identify a more clearly articulated theological framework for doing youth ministry. Kenda Dean, the director of the Institute for Youth Ministry at Princeton

Theological Seminary, is fond of saying that "youth ministry is first and foremost a theological task." I believe she is absolutely right. We do youth ministry because God calls us to be responsive to the particular needs of young people. And we respond in a distinct theological framework unique to youth ministry. I propose that there are five key theological tasks that we carry in youth ministry that are essential to a young person's growth in their faith.

❦

Theological Task One

To help young people know they are created by God and belong to God forever.

So God created humankind in God's image
in the image of God [God] created them;
male and female God created them. (Gen. 1:27).

❦

I praise you, for I am fearfully
and wonderfully made.

Wonderful are your works; that I know very well. (Ps. 139:14).

❦

Anna, at just over five months, certainly did not understand all that was happening. She was dressed in a beautiful flowing gown. Her parents, Ryoon Joong and Jack, took her to the front of the sanctuary along with their parents and friends. Pastor Chun said some words, and then Anna felt water on her head. She woke up startled and annoyed. Then the pastor used some oil and made the sign of the cross on her forehead. The pastor then walked her around the sanctuary, and as she looked around, Anna saw faces beaming at her. Anna was just baptized. And in years to come, Anna will relive her baptism through stories from her parents and others and through photographs. Whenever another child is baptized, Anna will be encouraged to remember her own baptism. In baptism, the truth we affirm over and over is that each of us is a child of God and is marked as God's own forever.

The creation story and *Psalm 139* remind us that we are created in God's image and from the beginning, God has a plan for us. Through the waters of baptism, we are marked as God's own and belong to God forever. As we grow, God has instilled in us particular characteristics. It is true that a fundamental developmental characteristic of adolescence is to shift primary allegiance from parents to friends. It is also true that a key characteristic of adolescence is to test the boundaries. For these reasons and others, ministry with adolescents presents unique challenges and opportunities. The church has long responded to the particular needs of youth and their families by creating youth ministry programs. But because adolescence is such a tumultuous time, all young people are at risk of potentially life-threatening behaviors. For all adolescents, but for young women especially, the single factor that contributes to young people engaging in "at-risk" behaviors is low self-esteem. Therefore, the task of youth ministry is to help build each young person's self-esteem. We do this by helping each one know to the core of their soul that they are created in the image of God and that they belong to God forever.

How do we live this task out in youth ministry?

• Youth ministry leaders authentically and consistently remind young people that they are created in the image of God. One of our associate pastors in North Carolina consistently refers to her young people by calling them "Image of God." Even when correcting someone she says across the youth room, "Excuse me, Image of God, I know you're not going to just leave that napkin on the floor."

• One youth group provided each of their young people with a small magnetized pocket mirror and framed it by writing each young person's name and "Image of God" around the edge. One of the leaders told me later he was surprised that most of them took their mirrors to school and put them on the inside of their locker door.

• I cringe when I visit a congregation whose youth ministry bulletin board features only young people who have won awards or scored highest in tests. I fear that we're sending the wrong message about self-esteem—that you are valued only for what you do and not for who you are. I encourage congregations to be sure that everyone is on the bulletin board.

❧

Theological Task Two

To help young people know they belong to the community of faith and must claim a place in the community.

I received a frustrated call one Monday morning. Jason had been disruptive again at youth group the previous night. Jason was described to me as a big thirteen-year-old who was too intelligent and mouthy for his own good. He wasn't liked by anyone and didn't seem to have friends. We talked about his background and what leaders had done so far. I affirmed all that had been done and encouraged a next step—a meeting with Jason with one adult leader and one of the youth leaders of the group. It was vitally important that they communicate to Jason their struggles with his behavior balanced with the truth that he is a part of their group—period. I encouraged them to read and study *1 Cor. 12:12–31* together.

Later I was told that Jason was a different person during the meeting. He was engaging and positive and apologetic. I encouraged both leaders to affirm Jason when he was doing the kinds of things that contributed to the group and to reaffirm his permanent place in the group. Several weeks later in a follow-up conversation, I was told that Jason still has his moments but that he was doing better. Further, the whole group had undertaken a study of *1 Cor. 12*, which was proving helpful for everyone.

❧

Now you are the body of Christ and individually members of it (1 Cor. 12:27).

❧

So then you are no longer strangers and aliens, but you are citizens with the saints and also members of the household of God, built upon the foundation of the apostles and prophets, with Christ Jesus himself as the cornerstone (Eph. 2:19–20).

❧

Youth ministry does not happen in a vacuum, nor can our faith in Jesus Christ live and grow in a vacuum. Because young people are developing their relationships with others, youth ministry depends heavily on community building and helping young people live together in a faithful community. Isolation and loneliness are common feelings in adolescents. Young people have told us they most often experience the presence of the Holy Spirit through others. In that way, the community becomes the incarnation of Christ, truly the body of Christ for others. We act in a powerful way as reflectors of Jesus Christ for young people. The light of Christ shines in us and is reflected to others. In the same way, young people reflect the light of Christ to us.

It is no secret that young people are on a desperate search for belonging. It is such a desperate search, in fact, that some form relationships with groups that devalue and harm them. Most gangs do an extraordinary job—sadly better than many of our congregations—of helping young people know they belong. Our task is to create a congregational atmosphere that clearly delivers the message to all young persons that they belong in this community and they have a place to claim here. Claiming a place means that young people are valued more than furniture. I shudder whenever young people are giving me a tour of their church building and when we pass a room, they say, "We aren't allowed in there. They're afraid we might break something." How can you belong when people put more value on the furniture than on you? Claiming a place means that you are valued now for who you are and the gifts you bring.

How do we live this task out in youth ministry?

• Many congregations are developing elaborate mentoring programs for young people who are going through confirmation. An excellent mentoring guide is provided in our denominational confirmation–commissioning resource *Journeys of Faith*.

Such a mentoring program engages young people in meaningful conversations with leaders in the church and helps young people know more about their community. Such knowledge helps them belong and claim a place for themselves.

• More than just carrying tables, when young people are called to particular responsibilities in the church, they experience both belonging and claiming a place. Not all young people are called to serve on the session (neither are all adults), but there are some young people who are called. When a young person is on the session, they serve as a powerful witness to all young people that they are welcomed and valued.

• After preaching in one of our congregations, I love to linger and watch which adults talk to young people and engage them in conversation, if only for a few seconds. Such conversations help young people know that they are a part of the community. Being known by name is a powerful thing.

❦

Theological Task Three

To help young people know that faith itself is a gift from God.

A group of Korean-American young people from the San Francisco Bay Area were on retreat, and on Saturday afternoon, we had a question-and-answer session. One of the young men raised his hand and struggled to ask a question. He said something like, "Well, what I want to know is . . . I mean, it seems like you're so sure and there's no proof and, well, how do I get faith?"

Before I could respond, the young woman next to him, looking incredulous, blurted out, "What do you mean? You just have to give your doubts to the Lord, that's all!" I'll never forget the look on his face. He turned to her in complete puzzlement and said, "What are you talking about?" It was a classic example of how God gives faith.

❦

Now faith is the assurance of things hoped for, the conviction of things not seen (Heb. 11:1).

❦

I am the vine, you are the branches. Those who abide in me and I in them bear much fruit, because apart from me you can do nothing (John 15:5).

❦

Because we claim the sovereignty of God, we Presbyterians also know that we do not get faith on our own. It is not as if we ourselves one day choose to believe just because we will it. We truly believe that "all things work together for good for those who love God, who are called according to God's purpose" *(Rom. 8:28)*. We do not get faith on our own. We Presbyterians do not believe in God in order to be saved. We believe in God because we have been saved. Ultimately, faith is a gift from God. And it will long be a mystery to me why God gives that faith more easily to some than to others. For some, like the young woman in the group I just mentioned, faith comes easily. It is easy to believe, to just know that God is and to give your doubts and worries to God and to know that God listens. For others, it is a profound struggle to believe in something you can't see and a God whose existence you cannot prove.

Still, our task is to help young people know that faith itself is a gift from God. And while we create communities and opportunities for the nurturing of faith, it is God who ultimately enables the growth and the insight to happen. Our task, then, is to prepare young people to be attentive to the Holy Spirit in their lives and to help them recognize how God is at work.

What does this task look like in youth ministry?

• Some of us have lost the gift of sharing testimonies and faith journeys. It is a wondrous thing to hear from others how they see God at work in their lives. Such witnesses to the work of the Holy Spirit enable young people to examine their own lives for similar growth and help them anticipate growth to come.

• Retreats are powerful settings for the work of the Holy Spirit. The opportunity to get away from distractions of everyday life and focus on your relationship with God can be a real gift and a soul-opening time. Consider a retreat centered on the spiritual disciplines and looking for God.

• Music continues to be one of the most powerful mediums for this generation. How does music express faith? Explore together how the different styles of music that youth value helps them be attentive to the Holy Spirit.

❦

Theological Task Four

To trust that the Holy Spirit gives us what we need.

I was visiting some friends several years ago and was delighted to be worshiping with them as their guest. I had been preaching several consecutive Sundays in different pulpits, and this was the first time in almost three months that I was able to be led in worship. I recall being excited and grateful for the opportunity to be a listener. Sadly, once the sermon began, I went into my critical mode. The content of the sermon, I thought to myself, was weak. This person had not done his homework. There was little imagination, and the delivery, I thought, was even weaker. In my arrogance, I walked out of the sanctuary disappointed and dismissed the sermon as one of the worst I had ever heard. I was surprised, therefore, when some weeks later I was prepping for yet another retreat when some of the words and ideas from that "awful" sermon came soaring through my soul. I remember stopping and shaking my head, thinking, "Nishioka, you think you know so much that you know what you need. But once again, thanks be to God that the Holy Spirit knows more than you will ever know and gives you what you need over and over." It is so true.

❦

And Abraham looked up and saw a ram, caught in a thicket by its horns. Abraham went and took the ram and offered it up as a burnt offering instead of his son. So Abraham called that place "The Lord will provide"; as it is said to this day, "On the mount of the Lord it shall be provided" (Gen. 22:13–14).

❦

And indeed [God] your heavenly Father knows that you need all these things. But strive first for God's realm and God's righteousness, and all these things will be given to you as well (Matt. 6:32).

❦

Lynn Turnage, who along with Bob Tuttle and me is writing this series of youth ministry resources, says that the greatest oxymoron of all time is "junior high leader." As usual, she's right. Anyone who has tried to "lead" junior highers and middle schoolers knows better.

Ultimately, the challenge for us as leaders is to place our trust in God and to do our faithful best. That's one of the reasons that serving as a youth ministry leader is so challenging; so much of our service is completely out of our control. In some ways, this is remarkably freeing. Because we do not have all the power we need in ourselves, we are forced to trust God. And in trusting the Holy Spirit, we are freed from focusing all that energy ourselves. Everything does not rely on us. It is the same message for young people. Our God provides for us. You don't have to do everything yourself. God is faithful, still.

For young people locked into a cycle that says they must do certain things or their self-worth plummets, or they must achieve to be successful, or they must whatever, this is an amazing message. It's not just you. God provides. The Holy Spirit is our advocate. Time and again we must be reminded that the Holy Spirit is more faithful than we will ever be and gives to us what we need— not necessarily what we want, but always what we need. Our fundamental task is to help young people see the ways in which the Holy Spirit is giving us what we need. In such a skeptical day and age, however, it is difficult to trust in that which we cannot see. The task of youth ministry is to help nurture young people's faith so that they can readily recognize and anticipate the faithfulness of the Holy Spirit in their lives.

How do we live this task out in youth ministry?

• Sadly, seeing God at work is a skill that has to be developed for most of us. For some, this comes easily, and for others, it is much more of a challenge. I encourage leaders to be on the lookout for God. Train yourself to be attentive throughout the day for signs of God's activity. When my youth group did a work trip in New York City for seven days, we ended each day sharing where we had seen God. By the middle of the week, we had so sharpened our senses that we were sharing "God-sightings" at every turn.

• Whenever you gather and share what has been happening since you last met (I call these highlights and lowlights), be sure to ask about how God has been active. Just as seeing God at work is a skill, so is talking about God. These conversations will also open questions about whether God caused something to happen or not. These are great lead-in questions to discussions about theology!

• Pray. Prayer is a powerful means and an amazing opportunity for us to be in contact with the Holy Spirit. Encourage everyone to pray. When we pray, we give direct attention to God and are in conversation with God. Praying is not perfect language or pretty words. Pray often and regularly with young people.

❧

Theological Task Five

To help young people become familiar and comfortable with the Bible, our best hope of knowing God.

Several years ago at a meeting of the Presbyterian Church's National Youth Ministry Council, we were studying the Bible and looking at what Scripture had to say about young people. We divided the council into smaller groups and focused on different passages in the Old and New Testaments. The study was a rich time of great discussion and discovery. When we finished, the two young people who comoderated the council, both seniors in high school, thanked me for leading the study, and both said they loved it. Then they shared that for both of them, this was their first time "studying the Bible." I was stunned. Here were two young people, bright, engaging leaders, who had grown up in the Presbyterian Church, and the *first time* they studied the Bible was as seniors at a national meeting. I probed deeper, thinking that perhaps they meant this was the first time they had studied the Bible in this way. (We'd used more of an inductive Bible study method.) No, they both assured me, this was their first experience at opening the Bible themselves and talking with others about what they had read and then applying what they had read to their lives.

❧

Your word is a lamp to my feet
and a light to my path" (Ps. 119:105).

❧

For all flesh is like grass
and all its glory like the flower of grass.

The grass withers,
and the flower falls,
but the word of the Lord
endures forever (1 Peter 1:24–25).

❧

Presbyterians are a people of the Word. The great shift in the Reformation for us was the movement of the focus of Christian worship from the Sacrament of the Lord's Supper to the preaching of the Word. It is ironic, then, that for many youth and adults in our congregations, the Bible receives so little attention. Pastors, church educators, and other church leaders need to remove the phrase, "you all know the story of . . ." from their vocabularies. The truth is, in any of our congregations, most of our people probably don't know the story, and every time we make that wrong assumption, we exclude and belittle them. We can and must do better.

Even among those who have grown up in our church schools, vacation Bible schools, and youth programs, we're finding that many have some familiarity with individual stories in the Bible, but few know where they are located or the overall order and sequence of persons and events. Further, because so much of our interpretation is done by others for us, we have little practice in asking what this passage has to do with me. Finally, for a visual generation, too much of the Bible, with all its wonder and colorful imagery, is simply read in unimaginative ways. Young people need to be engaged in the text in ways that help the text come alive for them.

How do we live this task out in youth ministry?

• At every opportunity, have young people work with their own Bibles and the text itself. Avoid printing verses for them. Encourage everyone to bring their Bible. If they don't have one, give one to them. And get into the habit of looking at verses together.

• Practice Bible study. Use the model provided in Chapter 6 of this resource. The hope is that the group will become so familiar with the process that they will begin applying it on their own.

• Tell stories and make no assumptions. Even when looking up a text, talk through the order of books of the Bible. Look at the verses. Glance at what is happening before and afterward. Set the context. Do this not by providing answers but rather by asking questions, such as, What's happening just before these verses? just afterward? Who is this being written to? by whom?

The Roots of Who We Are

4

The Five Intentions of Presbyterian Youth Ministry

While I was doing my student teaching at a high school in Seattle during my last year in college, my professor would come visit the class. At the end of the hour when we sat down together, she would look me straight in the eyes and ask, "What is the one thing you were hoping to teach this past hour?" At first, I babbled out a string of goals and ideas. Eventually, she helped me hone my teaching goal to a single key concept or idea around which the entire hour revolved. By the end of the semester, she began to quiz my students. At the end of the class session, she'd stand up, introduce herself, and then ask them to tell her what they thought I was trying to teach. Talk about a humbling experience! But throughout those months of evaluation, my very affirming and kind professor was helping me know that as a teacher, I had to have a clear concept or idea in my head. It is no less true for us in youth ministry.

In the later 1980s, the youth ministry staff and the youth ministry network began to develop five goals or intentions for youth ministry in Presbyterian churches. We tested these intentions and found congregations resonated with them. The hope of these intentions is to present to the church five clear goals or things we intend to do in youth ministry. Couched with the understanding of our Reformed theology, these five intentions provide clear, concise goals for what we are about in youth ministry in the Presbyterian Church (U.S.A.).

I contend it is critical that youth and adult leaders alike be able to respond to the question, So what is youth ministry all about at this church? If we babble a series of ambiguous and confusing statements, we miss an opportunity to both help people know the purpose of youth ministry and encourage them to participate.

Before we consider those things that we intend to do, it may help first to explain what we do not intend to do. Dave Ng, professor of education at San Francisco Theological Seminary, wrote in his excellent book *Youth in the Community of Disciples*[1] that when we do youth ministry, we do not intend to do the following four things:

1. *Maintenance.* We do not do youth ministry just to maintain young people through their adolescent years until they can contribute significantly to the congregation. Some people view youth ministry as glorified babysitting. Young people can sense this attitude in an instant. Such a view discounts the God-given gifts young people bring now and assumes they are of no value until they are older.

2. *Entertainment.* We do not do youth ministry to entertain and razzle dazzle young people. At first, I was envious of the kinds of programs that seemed able to bring in special speakers and great productions. These are not bad things in and of themselves but if we're trying to entertain young people, where will it stop? We simply cannot compete with the high-tech entertainment offered to young people today, nor do we need to.

3. *Protection.* We do not do youth ministry to protect young people from the world. In fact, Presbyterians, because of our Reformed theology, believe God calls us to be active in the world and to help bring about glimpses of God's realm. Young people cannot be protected from the world. Rather, our job is to equip them as disciples of Christ in the world to spread the good news of Christ's redeeming love.

4. *Fellowship.* This may sound strange at first, but Dave Ng's point is well taken. We do not do youth ministry to provide young people with an instant group of friends. Certainly we hope friendships will develop, but we are not just a nice social clique of people who get together to go on trips and watch videos. We are the body of Christ, called together by God and enabled by the Holy Spirit to witness to the world of God's love. So what do we do?

The Roots of Who We Are

The Five Intentions of Presbyterian Youth Ministry[2]

1. Call young people to be disciples of Jesus Christ.

Throughout the year, I typically am invited to our theological schools to teach a crash course on Presbyterian Youth Ministry. I was talking about the five intentions and this particular intention at Austin Presbyterian Theological Seminary in Austin, Texas, when one of the seminary students told me that it wasn't until seminary that he could remember anyone asking him about his faith in God and his relationship with Jesus Christ. I was stunned. I began, then, to ask the question about faith in God and relationship with Jesus Christ when I traveled to other theological schools and when I spent time with youth and adult leaders. I was surprised and disappointed to discover that significant numbers of youth and adults had never been engaged in a conversation about their faith while going through our churches, even through confirmation classes!

Our first intention, clearly, is that through the work of the Holy Spirit, young people would be called to be disciples of Jesus Christ. Remember that for us, the call comes both personally and corporately. We respond to the call personally by acknowledging Christ as our Lord and Savior, publicly professing our commitment to follow him, and then being obedient to God. We respond to the call corporately as members of the church. Being disciples together means caring for and supporting others, speaking out as the body of Christ against injustice, and proclaiming the good news to everyone through word and action. Responding to God's call to be a disciple means taking risks, meeting others' needs, putting God ahead of ourselves, and adopting a lifestyle that includes regular Bible study, prayer, worship, and service.

What does this look like in youth ministry?

Young people must be given a safe place in which to question their faith and to explore what it means to follow Jesus in their own lives. This happens through group building and Bible study, worship, and service. It happens through intentional conversations between adult mentors and young people about who Jesus Christ is and how the Holy Spirit is at work in each person's life. Adults must be free and open to share their own stories of faith with young people. Adults and youth alike must be held accountable to the call to be faithful disciples.

2. Respond to the needs and interests of young people.

I'm so grateful to youth ministry leaders who ask the question, Whose need is this really? Is it an adult need or is it a young person's need? Too often, I find that we adults impose our needs on young people. Some young people will tolerate this but almost always, it becomes a problem. I attended a weekend retreat for a presbytery in Alabama where the theme revolved around "understanding church structure." I did my best to keep the sessions interesting and we ended up creating an elaborate simulation game around our Presbyterian polity. We all learned a lot and the youth and adults enjoyed themselves, but more and more, as I worked with the Presbytery Youth Council, I began to get rumblings of discontent with the theme. Finally, I asked the hard question, How did you come up with this theme? Sadly, I discovered that one of the adult leaders had pretty much laid the theme on them and they agreed to it because they liked him so much. Through the grace of God, we did fine that weekend, but I could not help but feel how unempowered the youth council felt.

Young people come to the church with a wide variety of needs and interests. Responding to the those needs and interests is a critical component of youth ministry. It begins by recognizing each person as created in God's image and then by providing nurture and support for them. It continues in getting to know young people and inviting them to share their needs and interests. It's true that needs are very different from wants and that sometimes we truly don't know what we need. This is where the community comes in. Needs and interests must be tested in the community and clarified. Responding to needs and interests means raising hard questions. It is finding the balance between recognizing where young people are and offering a challenge and gentle push to encourage them to be their best. Responding to needs and interests means not only taking concerns seriously but also challenging young people to focus on the needs and interests of others.

What does this look like in youth ministry?

We respond to the needs and interests of young people whenever we build programs that respond to their particular concerns. It looks like talking about faith, love, friendship, relationships, hunger, peace, justice, sexuality, the media, and whatever. It looks like doing work projects and going on retreats and having lock-ins. It happens every time a youth leader meets and fully accepts a young person where they are rather than where the leader wants that young person to be.

3. Work together, youth and adults, in partnership.

The Snake River Mission Area includes the three presbyteries in Eastern Oregon and Southern Idaho. They work together to do much of their programming and share a common presbytery staff. I was invited to be the speaker for their week-long summer high school event. What I remember most about that week in Caldwell, Idaho (besides the fact that it was unusually hot), was the involvement of the young people as leaders with adults in every aspect of the conference. Everything from announcements to music leadership to dorm assignments involved young people. This was not an event where the adults stood idly by either. The adults were right in there too. When there was a conflict or a breech of the covenant, youth and adult leaders sat down together and decided what to do. The spirit of the week was amazing. I remember how easy it was to gain everyone's involvement. It felt very much like everyone was equally invested. I continue to hold that event and others like it as models for what it means for youth and adults to work together in partnership.

Youth ministry at its best is a partnership of youth and adults working together. It is adults doing youth ministry with young people, not to or for them. Partnership involves adults and young people together in everything from creating, to planning, to doing, to cleaning it all up. It is sharing experiences and visions with each other. It is trusting each other. People who take partnership seriously risk having to compromise and not always getting their own way. Partnership is hard work as well as team work.

What does this look like in youth ministry?

When you walk into a youth ministry program that practices partnership, you should immediately see that not only adults and not only young people but youth and adults together are leading. Partnership means that adults and young people have responsibilities for youth ministry but not necessarily the same responsibilities. Adults are partners with young people to provide help in getting events and programs planned, to share their faith journey with young people, and to provide a point of view as a person who has experienced things that young people have not yet experienced. Being a role model for young people means being willing to share with them, not lecture at them.

Young people involved in youth ministry are taking on new and more adult-type responsibilities. It is one step on their faith journey.

They count on caring adults to struggle with them, to help them look for answers, and to show them how faith is a part of one's whole life.

There is no question that partnership takes more time and more energy. But the rewards are amazing. And young people who have grown through a youth ministry program that practices partnership have told me they have developed skills for their whole life. One young person told me partnership meant that not just the adults clean up after a meal but that young people stay and help out. Another pastor told me that the greatest challenge he faces is letting go and sharing power. "But I realized it's basically an issue of trust," he said. "And I believe God is calling me to trust. When I frame it that way, it helps me let go."

4. Be connected to the whole church, community, and world.

It almost never fails that when young people give me a tour of their church building and then show me the "youth room," the room is one of the farthest and dingiest rooms on the property. There are exceptions to this, of course, and I'm grateful for them, but by and large this is the rule. I warn youth and adult leaders that in this location, it's easy to become isolated and when that happens, the congregation forgets whether they have a youth ministry program at all. The Presbyterian Youth Connection, our denomination's youth ministry organization in the United States, is built on the truth that young people really do want to be connected to each other, the church, and the whole world through faith in Jesus Christ. This fourth intention speaks to that truth directly.

Youth ministry cannot happen in a vacuum. It must be connected to the whole church. Our Presbyterian heritage connects each congregation to others through our presbyteries and connects our presbyteries to others through our synods and connects our synods to others through our General Assembly, and connects our General Assembly to others through our world ecumenical bodies. The connections go on and on! Youth ministry must also be connected to the world outside our churches. Presbyterian youth ministry is a part of the living body of Christ in all times and places.

What does this look like in youth ministry?

Many youth ministry programs are intentional about communicating what is happening in youth ministry to the whole congregation through newsletters and bulletin boards and special events. For a mission trip fundraiser, numerous youth groups invite congregational members to become "stockholders"

in the youth group event. When they return, stockholders
are invited to a dinner and young people tell of their experiences.

Youth ministry programs are connected to local schools when
pastors, church educators, and youth advisors visit campuses and talk
with teachers, coaches, and principals. Young people connect with
other young people through the Presbyterian Youth Connection,
through presbytery and synod events, and through going to
Montreat Youth Conferences and other conferences for youth
at our Presbyterian camps and conference centers and the
Presbyterian Youth Triennium. Such connections help young people
know they are not alone in their faith.

5. Be inclusive of all young people.

One of our larger, wealthier congregations in Atlanta was
struggling with their youth ministry program. They asked me
to visit and just observe what was happening. I was surprised to
show up at church school on Sunday morning and see most of the
young men dressed in light blue button-down shirts with khaki
pants and penny loafers and most of the young women wearing the
same style of dress. Two young men who were visiting that Sunday
were not dressed that way and were clearly ignored by the others.
The same was true for three young women who were wearing
slacks. The following Sunday, one of the young men had returned
and he, too, was wearing a light blue button-down shirt, khaki pants,
and penny loafers. The other young man didn't show up. Two of
the young women didn't come back. The third who did return was
wearing a dress. I asked the associate pastor where the dress code
was posted, and he had no idea what I was talking about. When I
pointed out the exclusive uniforms, he was surprised too because he
hadn't even noticed it.

Youth ministry is intended to be inclusive rather than exclusive.
We reach out to others, inviting them to belong to the community.
We affirm differences and celebrate commonalities. We seek to
include young people from many different cultures, belief systems,
and ethnic and economic backgrounds. Youth ministry is, like the
very nature of God, more interested in building bridges than walls.

Evangelism, sharing the good news of Jesus Christ with others, is a
critical component to this intention. We believe and because we
believe we belong to this community of faith. But belonging
ourselves is not enough. We also reach out to others, inviting them
to belong as well.

What does this look like in youth ministry?

First, remember that wherever young people are involved in the life of the congregation, youth ministry is happening. Youth ministry is not just a church school class or a youth group. God does not call everyone to grow in their faith in the same way and, therefore, not everyone is called to be in a youth group. (But everyone, in order to grow, needs to be involved in a community in some way.)

Second, cliques have no place in youth ministry. This is a particular struggle with so many young people from so many different schools in many of our congregations. Youth ministry leaders, youth and adults, need to work hard to break down cliques through intentional, faithful group building.

Finally, young people do need to be helped to share their faith with others. It is a natural thing for young people to invite their friends along on events and to youth group gatherings. Encourage it! Further, prepare your group to be open to these newcomers. The next chapter talks more about ways to help young people share their faith with others.

Discipleship, Needs and Interests, Partnership, Connected, Inclusive

Youth and adult leaders have shortened the Five Intentions to these seven words to make them more memorable. Consider posting these wherever and whenever you gather to remind you of the intentions.

Where Are You Strongest? Weakest?

Take time now to evaluate your youth ministry program. Given the Five Intentions, what do you do best? Where are you weak?

Under each of the intentions, list things that you do in your youth ministry program to meet that intention. Better yet, bring this task to a group of youth and adults and discuss it together. Once you have compiled your list, look at what you are doing. What might you do to strengthen areas where you are weak? to celebrate and build on areas where you are strong?

How Do We Do?

1. Intention: To call young people to be disciples of Jesus Christ.
   How We Carry Out the Intention:

2. Intention: To respond to the needs and interests of young people.
   How We Carry Out the Intention:

3. Intention: To work together, youth and adults, in partnership.
   How We Carry Out the Intention:

4. Intention: To be connected to the whole church, community, and world.
   How We Carry Out the Intention:

5. Intention: To be inclusive of all young people.
   How We Carry Out the Intention:

Ideas to further support the five intentions:

Evangelism for the Reformed Church

Yukon Presbytery sponsored an annual high school retreat beginning the Friday after Thanksgiving. I was there as the speaker. We were using an independently owned camp called the Gospel Victory Bible Camp, located a couple of hours outside of Anchorage. The theme for the retreat focused on discipleship in the midst of life's storms and the owners of the camp, an older couple, were pleasant and helpful as we settled in. They stayed to hear my first keynote session and were very complimentary. After the young people and other adults had been sent to small discussion and activity groups, the couple came up and asked to talk with me. They wanted to invite me back the next summer to lead a conference that they sponsored. I explained that my summer was already full with Presbyterian Church commitments. This intrigued them because they had heard that all of the mainline churches were dying. So we began to talk about my work, which led to their asking about my faith journey. The key question they posed was "When were you born again?" They both shared their exact days and times when they were born again and what happened, and then looked to me expectantly. I shared with them that growing up in a wonderful Christian home with God at the center, I could not recall a time in my life when I did not know that God had made me, that Christ had died for me, and that the Holy Spirit was with me.

The camp owners grew concerned and pressed. "But Rodger, when were you born again?" they asked. Then I explained that if they wanted a particular day I guess I would say at age seventeen when I was baptized and confirmed. But by this time they were clearly upset. "Are you telling us you haven't been born again?" they asked incredulously.

"No," I replied. "In fact, I am telling you that I have made a commitment to Jesus Christ as my Lord and Savior and have stood in front of my home congregation and said so. I believe truly that I am born again and again, moment by moment, by the grace of God."

I'll never forget their response. "Well, that's just not good enough!" the man said, and they both got up in a huff and left me sitting there. We continued to try and talk throughout the weekend, but clearly a wall had been built between us. They didn't sit in on anymore of my sessions and tried to talk to the pastor who was coordinating the weekend to share their concerns about me. When he told them a similar story about his faith journey, they didn't talk to him anymore either.

"That's just not good enough!" Those words still ring in my head. What saddens me the most, though, is the tone of judgment that was in the voice of the man. Sadly, that's the impression I think that most non-Christians have when they think of evangelism. They think of judgment and certainty and not being "good enough." I am thankful that's not the view we share as Presbyterians.

What Is Evangelism?

The Presbyterian Church (U.S.A.)'s evangelism program adopted the following definition of evangelism:

> Evangelism is joyfully sharing the good news of the sovereign love of God and calling people to repentance, to personal faith in Jesus Christ as Savior and Lord, to active membership in the church, and to obedient service in the world.

> Evangelism happens in youth ministry whenever the good news is shared. This happens when

> • Young people invite friends to lock-ins and ski retreats and those friends are greeted and welcomed in Jesus' name.

> • Youth and adults share together the struggles and joys of the past week and pray for and support each other, helping each one see God's faithfulness.

> • Youth and adult volunteers build homes with the help of the new occupants in Mexico, just over the border from McAllen, Texas, or in a neighborhood in Lawrence, Kansas. They are doing their best to be faithful.

> • A young person or adult advisor shares a personal testimony of how he or she grew to claim Jesus Christ as Lord and Savior.

Here are key theological concepts for Presbyterians concerning evangelism. At the heart of evangelism, the sharing of the good news, is a conversion. Because God calls us moment by moment to faithfulness, we Presbyterians believe we are converted by the Holy Spirit moment by moment. Literally, conversion is a turning. When we are converted, we turn our hearts once more to God. It is not that we are turning away constantly (although sometimes we are), but the Holy Spirit enables us to always be turning our hearts to God. What follows is a discussion of several key concepts for us as Reformed theologians when we look at conversions and evangelism, the sharing of the good news.

1. God Converts.

We must acknowledge that God, through the Holy Spirit, does the converting. We do not do the converting. Certainly we are called to faithfulness in helping young people see and understand their need for God, but the conversion is not our doing. It is God's doing. Presbyterians have a great history of "calls to commitment" and "invitations to discipleship." Even the "altar call" has a long history in the Presbyterian Church. But one of the greatest worries Presbyterians have about calls to commitment en masse is the tendency for manipulation and for the focus to be on the individual calling for the commitment rather than on God. Presbyterians also affirm a conversion that is more gradual (often called the nurtured conversion), where the individual cannot point to a particular time or place or event that jolted them to recognize their need for God, but instead, the person has known throughout his or her life of God's love and the power of the Christ and the Holy Spirit. Presbyterians affirm, too, the conversion that *does* revolve around a particular moment (often called the dramatic conversion) when a person is convicted in a powerful way to find love and forgiveness in Christ Jesus. To be sure, all Christians are called to stand before the community and profess Jesus Christ as Lord and Savior. But whether it be a nurtured conversion and confirmation or a dramatic conversion and going forward at a crusade, conversion, like salvation, is in God's hands.

2. We trust that things happen on God's timetable.

Sometimes I have met with adult leaders who deeply love the young people in their group and are so worried for them because some may have not yet professed a personal faith in Jesus Christ. In anguish, I have heard these adults say to me, "Rodger, if we don't get them to turn to Christ, we're going to lose them forever."

My response to these well-meaning adults is, "These young people will not be lost forever. God cannot be that heartless." I urge the adult leaders to continue to give the young people every opportunity to commit their lives to Christ, to continue to pray, and to continue to trust that God is at work in the young people's lives to bring them to conversion in God's time, not our own. It is a profoundly difficult thing to trust. But just as we claim God's sovereignty, we must remember that God is in control. We are not.

3. We provide opportunities for commitment.

I do worry that because we are so afraid of manipulation and emotionalism, all too often we neglect our young people in offering them the opportunity to know Christ as their Lord and Savior, to share their testimony of God's work in their lives, and to share the power of the Holy Spirit with friends. In our hesitancy, some of our young people are denied an opportunity to take an important step that they are ready to take and that they are yearning to take. That's why some of our young people go elsewhere.

Our experience tells us that commitments and conversions lead to deeper commitments and deeper conversions when they take place in a community of trust and care. Many of our youth groups do outstanding work in caring and building community, then we stop short of providing opportunities for young people to respond to the calling they are sensing from God. God converts on God's timetable, and we are called to provide the place and the opportunity for the conversion and commitments to be shared.

4. Commitments are a step in the journey.

One of the most disappointing and dangerous messages young people receive about conversion and commitments is that once you make them, it's all over. That's why ministries that focus only on the single commitment to Christ or the single conversion to Christ miss the point. That's not all there is. Presbyterians view conversion and commitment as lifelong. The phrase "God isn't through with me yet" is a sign and a promise. The sign is that God is at work in my life. The promise is that God will continue to be at work in my life. Certainly there are some conversions and commitments that are more profound than others. But no conversion or commitment is the end all. All are part of the journey.

How Do Youth Ministry Leaders Do Evangelism?

Stephen Jones, in his excellent book *Faithshaping*, outlines two specific behaviors for youth leaders to help nurture faith in young people. Jones tells us that we share the good news of the gospel through both nearness and directness.

Regarding "nearness," Jones says, "Being near to the faith and its traditions is pivotal to effective nurture with youth." He says nearness happens when

• Adults live out their faith in natural but expressive ways with young people.

• The young person feels she is an integral part of the church.

• The young person is encouraged to develop deep relationships with adult Christian models.

• Families express their faith.

• Adults verbalize their commitments.

• Youth experience how much faith is prized by adults who are significant in their lives.[1]

Regarding "directness," Jones says, "There must be specific times when the issues of faith are presented directly to young people." He says directness happens when

• The message of the gospel is presented in an appealing, fair, and open way.

• The focus on a decision is seen as only one aspect of the journey of transformation and conversion.

• Young people are offered a faith decision in relation to their maturity, life experience, and interest.

• Decisions happen on God's timetable rather than our own.

• We help youth address their own questions of faith.

• We give shape and focus to those moments when youth appear ready to open themselves more fully to God.[2]

I am more than impressed with how we nurture young people through nearness. I think we do that well. I am worried, however, about our work with young people in the evangelism that involves directness. Jones reminds us that our faithfulness is both nearness and directness, not either-or. The challenge for us is to present the good news directly to young people and to engage them in conversation about what that means for all of us. Many of our young people will eventually be confronted by people like the couple from the Gospel Victory Bible Camp. We do a disservice to our young people when we don't equip them with a response that is their own. I fear that some will hear the "that's just not good enough" phrase—and believe it.

6

Bible in Youth Ministry

The setting was an unscripted skit on the platform of Anderson Auditorium during the morning keynote of one of our summer youth conferences at our national conference center in Montreat, North Carolina. The two young women on the platform were holding telephone receivers up to an ear and were talking about coming to the youth conferences. One of them, Cindy, was a veteran and was trying to convince her friend, Jennifer, to come with the church group.

"You'll love it," Cindy said with enthusiasm. "We have so much fun!"

"Well, what do you do all day?" asked a hesitant Jennifer.

"Well, you start off in the morning with these things called energizers. Then we do singing, then we listen to a speaker, and then we go to small groups and talk about great stuff," explained Cindy.

"Well that doesn't sound all that fun," said an unconvinced Jennifer.

"But that ain't all," said Cindy. "I mean there are people there from all over. It's so cool. Everyone is nice and the guys—the guys are gorgeous!"

"Really?" said Jennifer, sounding a little more persuaded. "Well, I've never been to a church camp before. Do I have to bring a Bible?"

"A Bible?" said Cindy incredulously. "No you don't have to bring a Bible. This is a Presbyterian church camp!"

And with that, everyone in the auditorium broke up laughing, except me, of course. I was the one in the back of the hall crying. Sadly enough, while we Presbyterians are known as the people of the Word, for many of us, the Word remains a complete mystery.

When speaking to groups of young people, I remind them that we have no other way of knowing God than through God's Word given to us. That for us to know God best, we have to spend time reading and understanding the Bible. The good news for us is that we don't have to go through this confusing book alone. The Holy Spirit guides our understanding and, whenever possible, I encourage young people to study the Scriptures in small groups. After all, our Reformed theology says that no one has the corner on truth. Because we believe that, we study the Scripture together.

I'm grateful to the Rev. Juan Trevino, a gifted teacher and musician and copastor with his wife, Kathy (also a gifted teacher and musician), of a congregation in Texas. Juan developed and shared this Bible study model. I've adapted it some, but want to give Juan the credit for the outline and the ideas. My hope is that you will become so familiar with this model that as you and other youth and adult leaders use it, the steps will flow easily and you'll be able to focus more on the passage and less on the process.

Some words of advice:

1. This model assumes there is a group, preferably one that is no larger than eight people. It works best with narratives or stories in the Scripture. Texts that are straight forward, such as the poetry in the Psalms and Song of Solomon or the writings in Paul's epistles or Peter's or John's letters or John's revelation, are more difficult to study using this method. Parables also work well with this method.

2. Whenever possible, select a passage that is complete, in which the full story is told. Be aware, however, that early adolescents can best work with a shorter passage while older adolescents can work with longer passages.

3. Avoid printing Bible passages for study. Always encourage young people to bring their own Bibles and to read from them. If there are different translations, that's wonderful! Personally, I discourage young people from using the New King James, for instance, because the language is so difficult. There are excellent modern language translations available, such as the New Revised Standard Version, the New International Version, and the *Today's English Version*. I also discourage young people from using paraphrases of the Bible (e.g., *The Living Bible*, *The Message*, etc.) for study. Paraphrases are excellent devotional Bibles, but they are not translations and can be difficult when it comes to group study.

4. As you begin using this method, post a copy of it for all to see. In doing so, the group will begin to lead itself rather than always relying on one person to be a leader. (A group in Los Angeles has painted the steps on the wall of their church school classroom! Each Sunday, this is their process and the Bible is their curriculum. Youth and adults rotate responsibilities as facilitators.) Your major role as facilitator is to be sure everyone has had a chance to speak and to move the group to the next step when the group is ready.

5. Be comfortable as a group and have everyone on the same eye level. I discourage folks from sitting around tables. Tables feel too

much like school, which then gets us into the mode of trying to please the teacher and trying to guess the right answers.

6. For supplies, be sure everyone has a Bible. You'll need at least two sheets of newsprint and a marker or two. A study Bible and some commentaries would be helpful. *The Harper Collins Study Bible* (NRSV) is an excellent one. The new Interpretation Series of commentaries published by the Westminster John Knox Press is also highly recommended.

Ten-Step Method for Bible Study

Step 1: Pray.

If the group is gathering, start by sharing highlights and lowlights since the group last met. Open with prayer, asking the Holy Spirit to help you be attentive as you study God's Word.

Step 2: Read the passage.

Together read the passage. If there are different translations in the group, listen to each of them and note any differences.

Step 3: Visualize the passage.

Close your eyes and listen as someone reads the story again. Try to create a video screen on the back of your eyelids. Afterward, discuss as a group what people saw, heard, smelled, and felt during the reading.

Step 4: Reconstruct the passage.

From memory, try to reconstruct the passage by listing the events of the passage and recording them on a sheet of newsprint. When you think you have the passage reconstructed, look at the passage again to see if you missed anything or listed anything in the wrong order. Make any corrections as needed.

Step 5: Discover the context.

Share together the context of the passage as you understand it. If you have commentaries and a study Bible available, use these tools. What do you know is happening historically when this passage was written? Who wrote it? for what purpose? What is the tone of the passage? Where is the passage placed in Scripture? What happened just before this? What happens just afterward? You may need to do some background work in preparation for this step so you don't get bogged down here.

Step 6: Ask questions.

List any and all questions this passage raises for the group. Don't try to answer them. This is just a question-asking time. Be careful. It's easy to start answering questions, but the truth is that some questions are just meant to be asked. I encourage you to be in more of a brainstorming mode where any and all questions, no matter how bizarre, are listed.

Note: Another option here is to lead a discussion based on questions you may have already prepared. This moves the group quickly to Step 8. If you choose this option, be sure to invite group members to add their own questions and to return to Step 7 before moving to Step 9.

Step 7: Discuss the Big Three Questions.

All of Scripture says something about who we are and something about who God is and speaks to us from God. Take time now to discuss and respond to the Big Three Questions that follow. I hope you are able to reach consensus on what is being said here.

1. What does this passage say about people?
2. What does this passage say about God?
3. What is God saying to us through this passage?

Step 8: Respond to the questions.

Go through the questions the group generated earlier and discuss them. Remember that you don't have to answer all the questions! In my experience leading this process, groups may still have energy around some of these questions, but a lot of them are ready to move on, especially after discussing the Big Three Questions.

Step 9: Now what?

Discuss together how this passage has an impact on your life.

- What does this passage have to say to me in my daily life?
- How will it help me be more faithful as a result of our study?

These responses may be similar to some of the responses to the Big Three Questions. We hope the group will build on them. The intention here is to move from discussion to application.

Step 10: Close with prayer.

Close the study time with prayer. Invite group members to share prayer concerns before you close. Remember, there are a variety of ways to pray! Make use of circle prayers, with each person praying for the person on their right and asking one person to close the prayer.

7
V i s i o n   S t a t e m e n t

Years ago I was watching a Public Broadcasting television series titled "In Search of Excellence" based on the book by Tom Peters (Harper Collins,1982). Each episode focused on a different entrepreneur who had done well. The particular episode I watched focused on a young man named Steven Jobs who had grown his upstart Apple Computer Company into a multimillion dollar business. The interviewer followed Jobs around his company and interviewed employees and told about Jobs's childhood. Then at the end of the show, he talked directly with Jobs about how his leadership brought about the rise of Apple. The interviewer kept trying to get Jobs to articulate a secret or a formula for his success. Jobs seemed a little frustrated by this angle of questioning, and finally he turned to the interviewer and said, "OK, do you want to know what I did to make this company successful? I am the keeper and purveyor of the vision," he said. "Today, for any company to make it, somebody has to be the keeper and purveyor of the vision so that all they do is walk around and remind people why they're doing what they're doing."

Vision is the catchword for leadership. Jobs was right. In order to be successful, someone has to have a vision, and someone has to share it and remind people of it. It is no different for us. Today, in order for us to be faithful, we have to seek God's vision, and then we must constantly remind each other so that we keep the vision in front of us.

It was this kind of thinking that motivated the National Presbyterian Youth Ministry Council in 1989 to begin the process of discerning God's vision for youth ministry in the Presbyterian Church (U.S.A.). Along the way, several people asked me why this was so important.

A vision statement provides your destination. This is different from intentions and goal statements. Intentions and goals help you get to your destination. The vision *is* the destination. There is a proverb that says "If you don't know where you're going, you'll probably end up there." For years it had bothered me that we had nothing that clearly articulated why we are doing what we are doing. As the Intentions began to take hold, it became even clearer to me that we had to have a vision statement first.

Why not call it a mission statement? The mission statements I had read confused the concept of destination and the means to the destination. I was not interested in goals. Our intentions provided that well for us. I was interested in a statement that clearly articulated where we hoped to end up. Vision statements answer the "why" question. Goals and intentions answer the "how" and the "what" questions. As you read the vision statement itself, you'll see that language from the Intentions appears throughout. This ties the vision with the means to getting there. The vision statement itself is contained in the section that begins, "We have a vision of youth ministry in the church . . ." It is just over 150 words.

The Roots of Who We Are

A Vision for Presbyterian Youth Ministry
Adopted by the 202nd (1990) General Assembly
of the Presbyterian Church (U.S.A.)

As those involved in youth ministry, young people and adults, this is our vision:

We are children of God.

We are female and male, of all ages and conditions.

We come from many social, economic, and racial/ethnic backgrounds. As God's children, we are called into a loving relationship with our Creator, Redeemer, and Sustainer.

We experience God's love as the Holy Spirit leads us in the living of life.

We are Presbyterians.

We are part of the Reformed family of faith.

We experience God's love and grace through prayer, worship, service, the study of scripture and history, our participation in the church as the body of Christ, our partnership with people of other faiths, and our ministry of seeking justice for all people.

We are a vital part of the church and its mission. Through youth ministry, we are nurtured as the church responds to our needs and interests and as we give and share ourselves in the church's mission and ministry.

We have a vision of youth ministry in the church . . .

Where each young person is called to be
a disciple of Jesus Christ and is helped
to grow in a dynamic,
genuine and meaningful faith;

Where young people are involved
throughout the church's life and are
able to take risks in supportive
community without fear of rejection;

Where young people are educated within
their congregations and in institutions
both secular and sacred, and are

supported in their quest for truth and
knowledge in all disciplines;

Where youth and adults together as
partners create a community which
celebrates diversity and cherishes each
other's gifts;

Where youth are challenged and enabled to
respond to God's call to wholeness in
their lives and in the world; and

Where young people discover and claim over
and over again the Good News of God's
redeeming and sustaining love.

Vision gives direction to all ministry.

"Where there is no vision, the people will perish."
—Proverbs 29:18.

Without vision, youth ministry becomes lifeless.

This vision, which we claim, seeks
wholeness and life for all people as
children of God.[1]

As Presbyterians, our confessions and creeds form the foundation of our theology and faith. Our *Book of Order* is the heart and soul of our polity; our Directory for Worship describes our life in community, and the Bible, God's word to us, is one key measure of our faithfulness and witness. Words count.

Visions count. As God's people throughout time and history, we have been graced with visions. God's imprint upon history has often been initiated by a clear, singular vision. Where there is no vision, the people have been rudderless, wandering, lost. Visions count.

Recognizing the importance of a common vision and the need for words to express it, the youth and adults of the National Presbyterian Youth Council undertook the task of preparing a vision statement for youth ministry in the Presbyterian Church (U.S.A.).

The first draft of the statement was passed by the council in March 1989, at its meeting in Los Angeles, California. The statement was sent to the church for its reading and comment. Comments were received from individuals, youth groups, congregations, youth councils, and committees, boards, and agencies from across the church.

The statement was revised, and a final draft was passed by the National Presbyterian Youth Council in January 1990, at its meeting in San Antonio, Texas. The statement was then sent to the members of the Education and Congregational Nurture Ministry Unit Committee, the parent group of the youth council at that time. The Unit committee, in their meeting in March 1990, in Louisville, Kentucky, voted to recommend the adoption of the vision statement to the 202nd General Assembly of the Presbyterian Church (U.S.A.).

Finally, on June 2, 1990, the statement was brought before the General Assembly. Several youth advisory delegates spoke eloquently in favor of the passage of the vision statement. The statement was passed by the commissioners, and to the applause of the General Assembly, the Presbyterian Church (U.S.A.) had adopted its first vision statement on youth ministry.

The vision statement is ours. It belongs to us. It is a gift. It tells simply and clearly our hopes for youth ministry in the Presbyterian Church (U.S.A.). We hope this vision statement will encourage youth and adults in congregations, presbyteries, and synods to create their own vision statements for youth ministry.

Whatever happens and however this vision statement is used, no statement can ever be complete. Visions change. But if we do not share when we hear God calling us and if we do not seek confirmation from the community, then we will likely never get anywhere. We have a vision. Now we move on to discover more of the journey God has set before us. After all, words do count, and so do visions.

Creating Your Own Vision Statement

By now, I hope it's clear that each congregation needs to seek a particular vision statement for its own ministry with young people. If you are interested in doing so, use the following process as a guide.

1. Begin by gathering a group of interested youth and adults. After praying together, invite the group to open their Bibles to the book of Habakkuk in the Old Testament. Explain that Habakkuk, one of the minor prophets, preached at a time when the Babylonians were on the march and overrunning all the little kingdoms of the Middle East. Habakkuk is questioning the justice of God in allowing the Babylonians to triumph, and he finally receives the answer that "the righteous live by their faith." The whole book is only three chapters long. As a whole group, read the book through together.

2. Focus the group's attention on Hab. 2:1–3. On a sheet of newsprint or on a chalk board or white board, list the things we learn about vision from this passage. I propose four characteristics of vision.

A. Vision is given by God. Clearly, in this passage, vision comes from God. We don't generate the vision ourselves. We don't create vision. Vision comes from God when we are attentive to God's Spirit.

B. Vision is brief. The vision needed to be written so that a runner could read it. It's available to all people, and it is brief.

C. Vision is in God's time. We may become impatient, but a God-given vision will come about. It will happen.

D. Vision takes hard work and is practiced. Once a vision is given, we live into it. Habakkuk was active in his seeking the vision and even in his waiting for it. We don't just sit around. Vision takes work. It is practiced.

E. Vision is shared—tested by the community of faith. Clearly, the vision given by God is to be shared. Habakkuk isn't going to keep this to himself. One of the tenets of our Reformed tradition is that we are never alone. God is with us, and God calls us to be part of a community of faith. Vision must not only be personally felt but affirmed by the community for it to be authentic.

3. Distribute copies of the General Assembly's vision statement for youth ministry and read through it together. The vision statement really is the paragraph that begins, "We have a vision of our youth ministry in the church . . . "

Explain that this vision statement, written by the National Presbyterian Youth Ministry Council and approved by the General Assembly, forms the basis for the work of the council, and the vision statement written by this group will do the same for your congregation's youth ministry.

4. Hand out small file cards and ask people to take some time to listen for the Holy Spirit's leading. Then tell them to write down their responses to the question, As a result of our youth ministry, what do we hope happens with our young people?

After a few minutes, invite folks to share what they've written, either in the whole group, or, if the group is large, in smaller groups.

5. On a sheet of newsprint, invite group members to gather and write no more than five statements that they as a group feel *must* be included in a vision statement. Everyone must agree on the statements. Again, if your group is large, divide into smaller groups and give each group a sheet of newsprint. From here, you may want to select two or three people with strong writing skills to take the ideas of the group, including the cards, and to create a draft of a vision statement for your congregation's youth ministry.

This statement can be circulated among group members and other young people, parents, and congregation members for their comments. Eventually, the statement should be proposed to the session for adoption or to the congregation at a congregational meeting. Post the vision statement for all to see, and use it to evaluate all that you do. Remember Steve Jobs's phrase that someone or some group of people have to be the "keeper and purveyor of the vision"!

8
Characteristics of Young People

A pastor from Minneapolis told me he was chaperoning a group of his most mischievous middle-school guys at a presbytery weekend retreat. On their last night at the camp, he suspected his guys had plans to sneak out of the cabin late and raid a cabin full of girls. He lectured his group just before turning out the lights, and they promised they would behave. He intended to stay awake in his bunk just to be sure but he dozed off and woke to shrieks and screams from one of the girls' cabins. He ran outside in the pitch dark and nearly killed himself running into a tree. As he picked himself up off the ground, he saw flashes of middle school boys running past him back to his cabin.

"I was so angry," he told me later, "that my ordination vows were in serious jeopardy." He reached out his hands and snagged two of the boys before they got back to the cabin. He remembers backing them up against the side of the cabin and screaming at them, "What were you doing? Didn't you promise me you wouldn't sneak out? Why don't you guys act your age? Well? Well? Say something!"

To which one of his guys looked up at him, shrugged his shoulders and said, "Um. I was acting my age. I'm thirteen."

To his credit, the pastor realized that his early adolescent guys were indeed acting their age. In fact, he told me later that when those words came out of the middle schooler's mouth, he instantly flashed back to when he was in junior high at a presbytery retreat doing the exact same thing.

Too often we forget that young people are not adults, even when they are taller or stronger or seem to know so much more about life than we did at their age. Young people are complex bundles of hormones and energy. At no other time in their lives will they face more physical, intellectual, and emotional changes than during adolescence. These changes may happen slowly or rapidly, early or late, all at once or over a period of years.

Those of us who work with these amazing young people need to be aware that the individuals we are dealing with today are not the same as they were yesterday and certainly will not be the same tomorrow. As a leader, then, how do we cope? The first crucial step is to know and remember that all of this is within God's plan. I remind parents and stepparents that the God who made us all created us so that in adolescence we would begin to change our primary connections from our family to our friends. All this is in God's plan! The second step is to know and understand the kinds of changes that God has ordained for young people and the implications for our ministry with them.

The following charts describe some of the changes early adolescents (ages twelve to fifteen) and older adolescents (ages fifteen to nineteen) encounter in different areas of their lives. While there is no delineation between male and female development within each of the age levels, remember that there is a profound difference between genders. As a rule, young women tend to develop much faster than young men. Adolescence often starts as early as age nine in a female.

Remember, too, that any description of change in young people speaks in generalities. You know best the development patterns of each person. Gaining a working knowledge from these pages will help as you plan programs and cope with changing attitudes and behaviors.

Early Adolescents (Ages 12–15)

What is happening with early adolescents as they relate to others?

- Most begin to shift primary allegiance from family to peer groups.
- Belonging to a peer group and being accepted by peers gains more importance.
- Some begin moving from exclusively same-sex friendships to more friendships with the opposite sex.
- Most vacillate between dependence on adults and independence from them. Many have adult models and heroes, often mass media entertainment figures.
- Many act out racial, ethnic, religious,gender, and class stereotypes and prejudices formed at an earlier age.

Therefore, a faithful ministry with early adolescents must do the following:

- Ensure that time and energy are spent in developing a sense of community among young people.

- Provide opportunities for consistent and positive adult-youth interaction.
- Provide opportunities for positive, nonthreatening peer interaction.
- Break down divisive stereotypes, cliques, and prejudices.

What is happening with early adolescents and the family?

- Early adolescents experience distance from and conflict with their parents/stepparents more than they did as children.
- Some experience greater sibling conflict than in childhood.
- Many are living in family patterns other than with both biological parents.
- Peer and school activities consume more time and interest versus family activities.

Therefore, a faithful ministry with early adolescents must do the following:

- Provide opportunities for positive family interaction.
- Provide support for parents/stepparents.
- Recognize that not all early adolescents are living in traditional family settings.
- Help young people and adults gain skills in positive conflict resolution.

What is happening with early adolescents and physical changes?

- Most experience spurts of rapid growth and may be awkward.
- Physical appearance and attractiveness are much more of a concern.
- Some early adolescents experience rapid growth in strength, coordination, and athletic ability.

- Many experiment with different roles, varying widely in character, values, mood, and behavior.
- Most experience the onset of puberty.
- Most experience genital maturation, first menstruation or first ejaculation.
- Most gain full capacity for reproduction and develop secondary sexual characteristics (breasts, body hair, voice changes, etc.)
- Most develop sexual interests and fantasies and experiment with masturbation.

Therefore, a faithful ministry with early adolescents must do the following:

- Help early adolescents understand that the changes they are experiencing are part of God's plan and are normal.
- Avoid embarrassing individuals by calling attention to physical changes.
- Enable young people to recognize and learn more about their sexuality in a healthy, safe environment.
- Avoid activities that demand great coordination or agility.
- Recognize that role experimentation, value changes, and mood swings are part of growth.
- Accept individuals for who they are and who they are becoming.

What is happening with early adolescents and spiritual development?

- Most are beginning to question the literal faith of childhood while at the same time accepting a conventional faith.
- Some are moving into development of a more personal faith based on reflective thinking.
- The religious knowledge of most is spotty and poorly organized.

Therefore, a faithful ministry with early adolescents must do the following:

- Provide opportunities for questioning faith.
- Challenge early adolescents to begin to articulate what they believe.
- Enable young people to gain more biblical knowledge and organize it.

What is happening with early adolescents and intellectual development and learning?

- A few are moving from almost wholly concrete ways of thinking into more general, abstract, and symbolic forms of thinking.
- The reading level of early adolescents varies greatly.
- The vast majority are visual rather than auditory learners.
- Most learn better by doing than by watching.
- Most have short attention spans.

Therefore, a faithful ministry with early adolescents must do the following:

- Recognize that not all are capable of or comfortable reading aloud.
- Depend heavily on visual aids and active learning.
- Make allowances for frequent loss of attention.
- Include more concrete terms and images than abstract ones.

What is happening with early adolescents and self-esteem?

- Most experience considerable anxiety regarding personal identity and adequacy.
- Many females have low self-esteem connected to negative conditioning in earlier years.
- Self-esteem is tied more to doing than being and therefore fluctuates greatly.
- The search for sexual identity may cause conflict and confusion with parents/ stepparents.
- For most youth of Asian, Hispanic, Native American, African, and mixed race

backgrounds, ethnic heritage is greatly involved in the search for identity.

Therefore, a faithful ministry with early adolescents must do the following:

- Provide a safe place where early adolescents are helped to cope with anxieties about self-esteem, sexual identity, personal inadequacy, and racial ethnic heritage.
- Affirm each person as a child of God.
- Enable young people to develop a healthy self-esteem.

What is happening with early adolescents and characteristic behaviors?

- Many are exuberant, spirited, reckless, and energetic, especially in groups.
- Most have short attention spans and respond best to frequent changes in pace.
- Most are willing to experiment with new approaches.
- Many appear spontaneous, unpredictable, flighty.
- Many take a deep interest in popular music.
- Many spend long hours watching television and videos or playing video/computer games.

Therefore, a faithful program with early adolescents must do the following:

- Include frequent and often extreme changes in pace.
- Set, communicate, and enforce clear, fair, and firm behavioral expectations.
- Provide leaders who are patient and fair.
- Educate about drug and alcohol abuse and provide training in refusal skills.
- Model and teach critical viewing and listening skills.

Older Adolescents (15–19 Years Old)
What is happening with older adolescents as they relate to others?

- Most continue to pursue acceptance by peers; many find acceptance by a select peer group most important.
- Most late teens relate to both same-sex and opposite-sex friendships.

- Some begin serious sexual relationships.
- Relationships with adults vary from conflict to friendship. Authority becomes personified in adults (often in parents/stepparents) and, for many, becomes a threat to freedom.
- Independence becomes more important, with a greater emphasis on responsibility.
- Adult relationships, although conflictual, continue to be important, especially as friendships form and in times of crisis.
- Many continue to accept established stereotypes, but many others reject stereotypes, in an attempt to establish independence and new lifestyles.

Therefore, a faithful ministry with older adolescents must do the following:

- Ensure that time and energy are spent in developing a sense of community.
- Provide opportunities for positive adult-youth friendships to develop.
- Include adults who are willing to work with young people as partners.
- Enable adolescents to assume leadership roles and to develop skills as peer counselors.
- Work to question stereotypes and lifestyle issues.
- Help adolescents develop healthy one-to-one same-sex and opposite-sex relationships.

What is happening with older adolescents and the family?

- Conflict with parents/stepparents becomes more intense as each establishes his or her own identity.
- In the later years of high school parent/step parent-youth relationships may mellow.
- Some young people begin to form their own families through engagement, marriage, birth of children.
- Peer relationships, school activities, work,

and beginning careers become more and more important, consuming much time.

Therefore, a faithful ministry with older adolescents must do the following:

- Provide opportunities for positive family interaction.
- Provide support for parents/stepparents.
- Enable young people to realistically view their future as family members and possible parents
- Begin to teach parenting skills.
- Help young people and parents/stepparents as the relationship continues to change.

What is happening with older adolescents and physical changes?

- Some mature later than others and experience rapid growth as late teens. While this late development is normal, the delay is likely to be painful.
- Some are happy with their appearance and bodies.
- Strength and coordination become more manageable and reliable.
- Sexual interests continue to grow, with fantasies and experimentation becoming more frequent.

Therefore, a faithful ministry with older adolescents must do the following:

- Help young people develop a healthy attitude toward their bodies.
- Enable them to cope with their sexuality faithfully.
- Continue to educate them about the changes they are experiencing.

What is happening with older adolescents and spiritual development?

- Some are just now beginning to raise questions about religion.
- Many adolescents are attempting to put the pieces together for themselves.
- Many are trying to apply their faith to their lives and to see what difference it makes.

Therefore, a faithful ministry with older adolescents must do the following:

- Continue to raise questions about faith.
- Challenge them to articulate what they believe.
- Provide opportunities to apply faith to real world issues and situations.
- Provide opportunities for biblical and theological study.

What is happening with older adolescents and intellectual development and learning?

- Many are able to think abstractly and globally.
- Reading levels still vary greatly; many struggle to write coherently.
- Electronic media is even more important.
- More are able to concentrate for greater periods of time.
- Many are able to pay attention to a variety of media simultaneously.
- Most are more interested in discussions and sharing what they believe while hearing what others believe.

Therefore, a faithful ministry with older adolescents must do the following:

- Challenge them to think abstractly.
- Broaden their perspectives to include the whole church, community, and world.
- Depend heavily on the electronic media to convey messages.
- Provide opportunities for intense discussions and concentration.
- Avoid lecturing.

What is happening with older adolescents and self-esteem?

- Anxiety about personal identity continues for many, but others begin to accept who they are.

- Most older adolescents will select a role model who may or may not remain so in the future.
- The search for sexual identity continues.
- Many become personally aware of and concerned about ethnic heritage and cultural awareness.

Therefore, a faithful ministry with older adolescents must do the following:

- Continue to provide a safe place where young people may cope with anxieties about appearance, sexual identity, achievements, personal inadequacy, and other issues of self-esteem.
- Affirm each person as a child of God.
- Enable adolescents to continue to develop a healthy self-concept.
- Provide positive adult role models.

What is happening with older adolescents and characteristic behaviors?

- Most are settled, some to the degree of experiencing boredom, in groups.
- Most are willing to experiment, but many express reserve.
- Many are willing to take on responsibility and are capable of managing difficult tasks.
- Music interests continue to dominate. Some create their own groups.
- Drug use becomes widespread, but some become champions against the use of drugs.

Therefore, a faithful ministry with older adolescents must do the following:

- Provide opportunities to assume responsibilities within the group and the whole church.
- Provide outlets for music interests in the faith community.
- Help to relieve rather than create more stress in young people's lives by providing a strong community that is comfortable yet challenging.
- Include referral and counseling services for drug and alcohol abusers.

9

A Word About the Presbyterian Youth Connection

The Presbyterian Church (U.S.A.) has launched the single most exciting initiative in youth ministry in many years. The Presbyterian Youth Connection, the new youth ministry initiative for the denomination, is up and running and receiving widespread interest and support.

Who Is Included in the Presbyterian Youth Connection?

Presbyterian Youth Connection includes all Presbyterian Church (U.S.A.) youth and adults. "Youth" is defined as young people ages twelve to eighteen or those in the sixth through twelfth grades.

What Is the Presbyterian Youth Connection?

The Presbyterian Youth Connection is a common identity, theology, and design for youth ministry in our congregations. The Presbyterian Youth Connection gives youth from Maine to Hawaii and from Puerto Rico to Alaska a connection through a common identity. Not only do we all believe in Jesus Christ, as Presbyterian youth, but we share a common name and symbol.

The purpose of the Presbyterian Youth Connection is best stated in the mission statement:

As youth and adults, we respond to God's call through the Holy Spirit to be connected to each other, the church, and the world so that our lives proclaim with joy that Jesus Christ is Lord!

Where Does the Presbyterian Youth Connection Happen?

Everywhere! The Presbyterian Youth Connection is based in congregations and clusters of congregations and includes connections to presbyteries, synods, and the General Assembly. The Presbyterian Youth Connection happens wherever and whenever young people are in ministry in the name of Jesus Christ!

When Did This All Get Started?

The Presbyterian Youth Connection is new. In fact, the Presbyterian Church (U.S.A.), including its predecessor denominations, has been without a youth ministry organization for nearly thirty years. The PYC was officially started with presentations at the General Assembly meeting and the Presbyterian Youth Triennium in July 1995.

Why Start the Presbyterian Youth Connection?

The Presbyterian Youth Connection grew out of an overture from congregations in Wyoming Presbytery asking for a new way to connect young people to each other across the church. The General Assembly asked the National Presbyterian Youth Ministry Council to create a study to see if other congregations supported Wyoming Presbytery's request for a new youth ministry organization.

What Were the Results of the Study?

The study conducted by the National Presbyterian Youth Ministry Council resulted in the identification of three major needs across the church. Young people in congregations raised the crucial needs for identity, belonging, and leadership opportunities.

1. *Identity*—A major task of adolescence is to begin to form answers to the questions, Who am I and what am I doing here? Young people are trying to figure out who they are, what they value, and how their lives have meaning. They are turning to the church to help them discover what it means to be a child of God and how they can live faithfully as disciples of Jesus Christ.

2. *Belonging*—It was clear from the study that significant numbers of young people in our congregations felt they did not belong. The congregations where youth ministry was thriving, whether it was a group of eight or eighty, were congregations where young people felt they belonged, where they felt they were important to the ministry of Jesus Christ. Young people identified a profound need to be accepted by other youth and adults.

3. *Leadership*—The third need stated by young people across the church was for leadership opportunities. Time and again, when young people were included in leadership, the commitment of young people to the church and the church's commitment to young people grew. Young people said they were ready to participate as leaders in the church today as well as in the future.

In response to these needs, the National Presbyterian Youth Ministry Council recommended the formation of a new youth ministry organization to be named "Presbyterian Youth Connection." The General Assembly approved the recommendation and the Presbyterian Youth Connection was born!

What Will All This Cost?

The Presbyterian Youth Connection is funded through the churchwide Pentecost offering, General Assembly mission dollars, sales of resources, and contributions from individuals, congregations, presbyteries, and synods.

What Do We Do To Join?

Call the Presbyterian Youth Connection office and request a packet of information on joining the Presbyterian Youth Connection. You'll be sent a step-by-step guide as well as a video and other information. Call 502-569-5499.

What Resources Are Available To Support Congregations?

One of the most significant benefits of the Presbyterian Youth Connection is a new generation of youth ministry resources for Presbyterian congregations. New resources include a guide for congregations, program designs for middle school youth groups, program designs for high school youth groups, a guide for synods and presbyteries, and a songbook with a CD and cassette. Call 502-569-5499 to request the *Presbyterian Youth Ministry Resources Catalog*, which features the new Presbyterian Youth Connection resources and includes order information and prices.

Note to you who are not members of the Presbyterian Church (U.S.A.):

Greetings, friends! This chapter focuses on the Presbyterian Youth Connection, which is the exciting new youth ministry initiative for the Presbyterian Church (U.S.A.). While the new resources may be helpful to you (especially the program designs for middle school and high school youth groups), the plan focuses exclusively on the PC(USA). Don't despair, however! Your national church offices offer great support for youth ministry! Call them and talk with them. If you don't know whom to call, talk with your pastor or church educator for contact persons, phone numbers, and e-mail addresses.

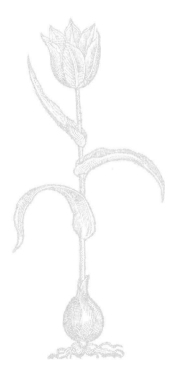

Notes

Chapter 1: Reformed Theology

    1. References to John Calvin's *Institutes* are from Calvin: *Institutes of the Christian Religion*, 2 vols., ed. John T. McNeill, trans. Ford Lewis Battles (Philadelphia: The Westminster Press, 1960). This first reference is found in Book I, ch. XIII, no. 20, p.146.

    2. Calvin, *Institutes*, Book IV, ch.VIII. no. 8, p. 1155.

    3. Calvin, *Institutes*, Book III, ch. XXI, no. 3, p. 924.

    4. Calvin, *Institutes*, Book III, ch. XIV, no. 17, p. 784.

    5. Calvin, *Institutes*, Book III, ch. XXII, no. 5, p. 937.

    6. Calvin, *Institutes*, Book IV, ch. I, no. 9, p. 1023.

    7. Calvin, *Institutes*, Book II, ch. II, no. 17, p. 276.

    8. Calvin, *Institutes*, Book II, ch. III, no. 8, pp. 300–301.

Chapter 2: Reformed or Not Reformed?

    1. Calvin, *Institutes*, Book IV, ch. XV, no. 20, p. 1321.

    2. Johanna W. Van Wijk-Bos, *Reformed and Feminist* (Louisville: Westminister/John Knox Press, 1991).

    3. St. Augustine, *City of God.*

    4. John Leith, T*he Reformed Imperative* (Louisville: Westminster/John Knox Press, 1987).

Chapter 4: The Five Intentions of Presbyterian Youth Ministry

    1. David Ng, *Youth in the Community of Disciples* (Valley Forge: Judson Press, 1984), p. 15.

    2. *Presbyterian Youth Guide* book, p. 9.

Chapter 5: Evangelism for the Reformed Church

    1. Stephen D. Jones, *Faith Shaping* (Valley Forge: Judson Press, 1987).

    2. Ibid.

Chapter 7: Vision Statement

    1. "A Vision Statement for Youth Ministry in the Presbyterian Church (U.S.A.)" adopted by the 202nd General Assembly (1990) of the Presbyterian Church (U.S.A.).

About the Writer

Rodger Nishioka is the coordinator for youth and young adult ministries in the Christian Education program area of the General Assembly Council of the Presbyterian Church (U.S.A.). An elder at the Church of Christ Presbyterian in Park Ridge, Illinois, Rodger also is a full-time student at McCormick Theological Seminary in Chicago. He is studying for a Master of Arts in Theological Studies and plans to pursue a Ph.D. in religious education. Rodger served as the associate for youth ministry with the General Assembly and taught English and social studies at Curtis Junior High School in Tacoma, Washington. Rodger enjoys the outdoors, visits to the beach, and eating sushi.